Under Stately Oaks

Under Stately Oaks

A PICTORIAL HISTORY *of* LSU

Text by Thomas F. Ruffin

Photography Research and Editing by Jo Jackson and Mary J. Hebert

Foreword by Mark A. Emmert, Chancellor

Preface by Laura F. Lindsay and J. Michael Desmond, for the University Commission on the History of LSU

Louisiana State
University Press

Baton Rouge

Copyright © 2002 by
Louisiana State University Press
All rights reserved
Manufactured in Hong Kong
First printing

11   10   09   08   07   06   05   04   03   0 2
5   4   3   2   1

Designer: Laura Roubique Gleason
Typeface: Minion
Printer and binder: Dai Nippon Printing, Inc.

Library of Congress Cataloging-in-
Publication Data:

Ruffin, Thomas F.
  Under stately oaks : a pictorial history of
LSU / text by Thomas F. Ruffin ; photography
research and editing by Jo Jackson and Mary J.
Hebert.
       p. cm.
Includes bibliographical references (p.   ) and
index.
  ISBN 0-8071-2682-9
  1. Louisiana State University—History.
  2. Louisiana State University—History—
Pictorial works. I. Jackson, Jo. II. Hebert,
Mary J. III. Title.
  LD3114.5 .R84 2001
  378.763'18—dc21

  2001002209

for Carol Baker Ruffin

Contents

Foreword

When the Seminary of Learning opened its doors in 1860, its founding fathers had a distinct vision for what would become Louisiana State University and Agricultural and Mechanical College. But even with their visionary enthusiasm, that corps of community leaders, politicians, and educators would most likely be amazed with the remarkable development of one of the nation's leading universities.

This pictorial history documents LSU's story of growth and transformation. It portrays the university's symbiotic relationship with the people of Louisiana through major historical episodes. Its academic, military, and athletic traditions have successfully created a community of shared experience and pride that ties LSU to all those who have walked its grounds. Each building, walkway, and field has its own story, from the Pentagon Barracks to the expression of social movements at Free Speech Alley.

This book also pays homage to legendary figures who were committed to establishing an exceptional university. The images captured in this work are portraits of events that have brought LSU to the twenty-first century. It traces the university's rich tradition of scholarship, evoking the intellectual genius of Robert Penn Warren and Cleanth Brooks, founders of the prestigious *Southern Review,* Eric Voegelin, one of the foremost minds in American philosophy, and noted historian T. Harry Williams.

Images of both everyday life and amazing events, these pictures convey the excitement and enthusiasm LSU students have always brought to our campus. This work also illustrates the service LSU has provided as a catalyst for economic and social success in the state.

Echoes of our history can still be heard across the campus, resonating the challenges and triumphs of the past as these are answered by an unabated vision of excellence for the future. The standards of intellectual rigor set down by earlier academic leaders are carried on in research laboratories, studios, and libraries. Indeed, the scholarship of LSU's faculty has never been stronger, and the energy and industry of its students are resulting in unprecedented academic success. Today, LSU inspires a new corps of innovators and thinkers while continuing its traditions and remembering its legacies.

These glimpses of the past illustrating the emergence of a great university will undoubtedly captivate readers. I know you will enjoy this visual narrative of LSU, an extraordinary university with a history of distinction.

Mark A. Emmert
Chancellor

Where stately oaks and broad magnolias
shade inspiring halls,
There stands our dear old Alma Mater
who to us recalls
Fond memories that waken in our hearts
a tender glow,
And make us happy for the love
that we have learned to know

All praise to thee our Alma Mater,
molder of mankind,
May greater glory, love unending
be forever thine.
Our worth in life will be thy worth
we pray to keep it true,
And may thy spirit live in us forever, L S U

—Harris Downey, 1928

Preface

It was over six years ago that the University Commission on the History of Louisiana State University and Agricultural and Mechanical College discussed the possibility of telling the LSU story. Although books about David and Thomas Boyd and other notable individuals with ties to LSU had been written, no one had attempted to write a comprehensive history since Walter Fleming's book, *Louisiana State University: 1860–1896*, was published in 1936. And so much has happened since the turn of the century: The first class of women (the "sensational 17") enrolled in 1906, the university moved from downtown Baton Rouge to its current site, segregation ended, enrollment expanded from under five hundred to over thirty thousand students, and the university budget increased from slightly over $100,000 to more than $275 million.

Funds were tight in 1995, and the minimal cost of producing a pictorial history was estimated at $25,000. For many folks with love and commitment to the "Ole War Skule," this was not a barrier. Discussions with Les Phillabaum of LSU Press, Tom Ruffin, an LSU alum who fits the often-professed description "bleeds purple and gold" and who had written many interesting articles for *LSU Magazine,* and Jennifer Cargill, Dean of the LSU Libraries, resulted in an agreement to produce a pictorial history of LSU through 2000–2001. At the same time, the Commission was able to take several additional steps toward our overall goals of producing a comprehensive history and preserving the university's heritage. We are extremely grateful to Commission member and chancellor emeritus Paul Murrill and his wife, Nancy, who together have established a professorship to support continuous faculty guidance and research for the production of a complete history. And we are pleased to have that research initiated under the direction of Professor Paul E. Hoffman, also a member of the Commission and of the LSU Department of History.

The record of accomplishments that this history chronicles is paralleled by the remarkable and distinctive beauty of the present LSU campus. In the year 2000–2001, we celebrated the 75th anniversary of the dedication of this campus on April 30, 1926. The many events for the celebration of the Jubilee year included commissioning a master plan for future campus development. This master plan assures that the university's plans for the future work hand in hand with the preservation and appreciation of its past.

As we reflect on the discussions that preceded these endeavors, we are saddened to observe that some of the members of the Commission who had the wisdom and vision to begin the process are no longer with us: Pete Taylor, chancellor emeritus, whose dedication to this university is unmatched; Mark Carleton, nationally noted historian, member of the faculty, and former chair and historical anchor for the Commission; and Pete Soderbergh, former dean of the College of Education and faculty member, who originated the idea of a pictorial history and published a history of the LSU Union. Others like Margaret Jameson can no longer participate in our dialogue. But their shared knowledge about LSU was tremendous, and all the more reason that we should continue to capture the memories while we can.

It was thrilling for us to see this project reach fruition in the Jubilee year. Now welcome to the table; enjoy the feast!

Laura F. Lindsay
J. Michael Desmond
University Commission on the History of LSU

Introduction

The history of Louisiana State University is closely tied to the history of Louisiana. The highs and lows, the troubles and victories of the state have always been reflected on campus. Louisiana has a fascinating, colorful, messy history full of intrigue and strong personalities. So does LSU.

Once the Seminary of Learning of the State of Louisiana was established in 1853, the founding fathers accepted the difficult task of building a campus in the piney woods of Central Louisiana. They confronted many setbacks, but when they did, they redoubled their efforts until they succeeded. Not only did they complete the seminary, they initiated a disciplined military curriculum on the order of West Point's. Then they selected retired major William Tecumseh Sherman to carry out the job. And he did.

A distinctive LSU spirit had already begun to evolve out of the seven-year struggle to create an institution of higher learning. By opening day, the seminary had also begun to cultivate its "Ole War Skule" heritage. Rooted in a military tradition and quickly known for training resilient soldiers, the institution proved to be a survivor.

That LSU spirit has overcome great odds. By the end of the second year, those students old enough had enlisted in the Civil War—one in the Union army, the balance in the Confederate forces. Some, because of their seminary training, became officers while still in their teens. LSU survived the political turbulence of Reconstruction, where native Democrats fought Radicals, carpetbaggers, scalawags, and others operating in the protective shadow of Union bayonets. And none of them stopped bickering long enough to fund a deserving school.

After a fire destroyed the school in 1869, resourceful leaders quickly found it a temporary home in Baton Rouge. When the legislature cut off LSU's funding during the 1870s, enrollment dipped to single digits. Only the Boyd brothers remained to teach.

Later generations encountered their own challenges and opportunities—among the many, the merger with the A&M College, two moves to new campuses, coeducation, the era of Huey P. Long, the notorious scandals of 1939, World War II, desegregation, the anti-Vietnam War protests, and periodic economic crises.

Yet these changes, as crucial as they were, did not impact LSU nearly so much as how the university community faced them and ultimately earned for the school its designation as Louisiana's flagship university. Eventually the shady splendor of LSU's magnificent live-oak trees nurtured generations of people who embody the spirit of LSU, and this is their story.

THE FIRST LAND GRANTS

"I fear that if education be left entirely to the patronage of the inhabitants, it will continue to be neglected; for they are not sufficiently informed to appreciate its value." —William C. C. Claiborne, new governor of Orleans Territory, in a letter to President Thomas Jefferson.

His concern was justified. Louisiana was the eighteenth state to enter the Union, and the first never to have been a British colony. The British settlers opened several colleges prior to 1776, nine enduring to this day. But Louisianians had a different mindset. Theirs was a paternalistic society where the colonists acquiesced to the wishes of the French, and after 1766, the Spanish rulers, who showed little interest in educating the common man. Hence Louisiana failed to start a single college, private or public, during its entire colonial period, which ended with the 1803 Louisiana Purchase.

Fortunately, the federal government had already taken steps that would benefit Louisiana. The Northwest Ordinance of July 1787 emphasized "schools . . . shall forever be encouraged" and came up with the means—the public domain. The first sixteen states retained ownership of their public lands. But in thirty of the thirty-four later states, including Louisiana, title to these lands remained in the hands of the federal government. As for these thirty, known as public land states, the United States used the acreage to stimulate everything from homesteading to railroads to, above all, education.

In 1803 Ohio became the first public land state to enter the Union. In 1812, Louisiana became the second. By 1860 there were fifteen public land states. Each received at least two townships of federal land within its borders—a total of seventy-two square miles, or 46,080 acres—for seminaries of learning or universities. Ohio promptly used its grants to open Ohio and Miami universities. Others followed with schools such as Indiana University and the Universities of Wisconsin, Michigan, Mississippi, Alabama, Iowa, and Missouri. But Louisiana lagged behind. Ground was finally broken at the Pineville site north of Alexandria in January 1856, and the Seminary of Learning of the State of Louisiana opened in 1860.

I | THE MILITARY SCHOOL

1   Sherman in Command

General William Tecumseh Sherman is well remembered for his declaration that "War is Hell!" Those thousands of families left homeless by his ruthless 1864–65 "march to the sea" readily agreed. The wanton destruction from Atlanta to South Carolina, whether caused by poorly disciplined Union troops acting on their own or from direct orders, embittered the South more than all the other Civil War clashes combined.

William Tecumseh Sherman

But lost in the intersectional hostility surrounding the general was the memory of his crucial role as an effective and inspiring educational leader.

The original board, the Board of Trustees, built the school. Now it was up to the school's new governing body, the Board of Supervisors, to run it. The group met for the first time three days before Christmas 1858, only to find itself facing $60,000 in debt with nothing to show for it—no money, building, textbooks, classroom furniture, laboratory equipment, library, faculty, or students. Whatever it needed to do in order to open, the board had only the calendar year 1859 in which to do it. This included hiring its first superintendent—not just any superintendent, but one who would establish the standards for generations to follow.

By law, the governor served as board chairman. The supervisors selected George Mason Graham as vice-chairman. They also picked an executive committee to make the day-to-day decisions and to contact other college presidents and professors to help develop a course of study. The supervisors focused on the two schools of greatest interest to the board—Virginia Military Institute, with its military tradition, and the University of Virginia, which took a more classical ap-

Louisiana State Seminary of Learning and Military Academy, Pineville, ca. 1868. Lithograph by Professor Samuel Lockett, who taught there during the post–Civil War period.

Facing page: George Mason Graham, "Father of LSU"

1845

New state constitution authorizes a seminary of learning to be financed by the interest accruing from the sales of lands donated by the federal government specifically for that purpose.

1852

A special commission selects the seminary site—the 438-acre farm owned by Elizabeth Routhe Williams, just across the Red River from Alexandria.

D.F. BOYD

POWHATAN CLARKE

GEN. WM. TECUMSEH SHERMAN

FRANCIS W. SMITH

ANTHONY VALLAS

The Seminary's original faculty included: Professor David French Boyd (top left), Superintendent William T. Sherman (center), Commandant of Cadets and Professor Francis W. Smith (bottom left), Professor Anthony Vallas (bottom right), and Professor E. Berté St. Ange (not pictured). Soon joining the group was Surgeon and Assistant Professor John W. Sevier (not pictured), who resigned in February 1860 and was replaced by Powhatan Clarke (top right).

proach to education. Once determining its direction, the board could then seek suitable candidates for its first president of the faculty.

By its second meeting, in May 1859, the board had heard from the two Virginia colleges. Board members were split over which model to adopt. But Graham favored VMI, and, with the governor's backing, he prevailed.

The board advertised in Washington, D.C.'s *National Intelligencer* and other publications to fill the five faculty spots. The board selected four professors from the eighty-one applicants: David French Boyd, who had attended the University of Virginia; Anthony Vallas, a Hungarian; E. Berté St. Ange, a Frenchman; and Francis W. Smith, a twenty-two-year-old graduate of VMI and the University of Virginia, who would also serve as commandant of cadets. William Tecumseh "Cump" Sherman, a native of Ohio and a graduate of the United States Military Academy, was selected to serve as superintendent.

Major Don Carlos Buell, a close family friend of Graham's, recommended Sherman. The absence of a teaching background seemed not to matter. Nor did the lack of success in the professional arena. In the Army, Sherman served in the Mexican War, but saw little action. In banking, he failed. And as a lawyer, he lost his only case. Still, Buell's endorsement was enough for Graham. And Graham's backing was enough for the board.

A congenial, auburn-haired, thirty-eight-year-old professional soldier, the new superintendent had graduated sixth in his class at West Point. After his father's death at an early age, Sherman was reared, but never adopted, by a family friend, Thomas Ewing, whose daughter Ellen he later married. She and their children planned to join him once he found suitable housing.

En route to Rapides Parish, the politically astute Sherman stopped first at Baton Rouge to visit Governor (and seminary board chairman) Robert C. Wickcliffe, then to Bayou Robert, just south of Alexandria, to call on Governor-elect Thomas O. Moore, and finally to Tyrone Plantation on Bayou Rapides, north of Alexandria, to confer with Graham. Reaching the campus in November 1859, Sherman found the structure "very large and handsome."

To meet the opening-day deadline, a mere month and a half away, Sherman's organizational skills came to the fore. The determined major hired local carpenters to make mess tables and benches, ordered furniture and text books from New Orleans, prepared a code of conduct and completed the curriculum. He added two new men to the seminary staff, Bernard Jarreau as steward and Dr. John W. Sevier as surgeon and assistant professor of ancient languages.

Sherman wrote the promotional circular for Governor Wickcliffe's signature, detailing the advantages of the seminary and listing the requirements for admission. "The Military System is not necessarily designed to make soldiers," he emphasized, but it teaches "the subordination to the laws . . . the use of arms and the science of organization" while exerting "a wide and wholesome restraint over young men."

Most of these early students lacked any formal education, though they were expected to be able to read and write correctly and to be familiar with the basic rules of arithmetic. Applicants were to be between the ages of fifteen and twenty-one.

When school opened on January 2, 1860, students began arriving from all parts of the state. By the end of the first day, nineteen students were on hand. One even came by horseback from Ouachita Parish, over one hundred miles away. And they kept coming, some in no hurry, until enrollment hit seventy. Some paid tuition, others were accepted without charge, having been appointed as state or beneficiary cadets.

The cadets found Sherman strict during school but relaxed after hours, often engaging them in informal chats. The major always addressed the students by name, putting them at ease in conversation. One possible shortcoming for them was his alert mind; he stayed a step or two ahead of anyone trying to outwit him. Sherman found that none of the students were sufficiently advanced for his engineering courses, so he turned to teaching history, usually discussing his favorite topic—the winning of the American West.

The students' greatest complaint, with justification, was the poor food, resulting in nighttime student foraging parties to the nearby farms for supplemental provisions. Neighbors complained about cadets stealing their chickens. This led to another grievance, discipline. Dispensed by Smith but backed by Sherman, discipline, some cadets claimed, was doled out unevenly. It must be kept in mind, though, that the students ranged from the highly motivated to the recalcitrant. Initially heavy, opposition to the military regimen softened after the arrival of the snappy new blue cadet uniforms with plumed hats.

The school had been established by the General Assembly in 1853 as the Seminary of Learning of the State of Louisiana. Sherman joined with Graham in pushing for a name change to the Louisiana Military Academy to emphasize the seminary's primary mission.

Residence of General Zachary Taylor on the downtown campus when he was elected president of the United States in 1848.

1853	1854	1855	1856
The General Assembly establishes the Seminary of Learning of the State of Louisiana, naming a board of trustees as its governing body.	The board of trustees holds its first meeting, naming George Mason Graham, later called the "Father of LSU," as its first chairman.	The Assembly directs the trustees to begin construction following the plans prepared by architect Alexander T. Wood.	Construction begins, using brick produced in primitive on-site kilns with clay excavated from school property. Tower wall collapses, causing major delay.

BATTLE OF THE BOARDS

In 1854 Governor Paul Hebert appointed a seven-man Board of Trustees to carry out the assembly's dictates—purchasing the property, erecting the buildings, selecting the curriculum, naming the faculty, running the school—and relying solely on interest from the seminary fund to do so.

The new board got off to a slow start. Only one of the seven members showed up for the scheduled June 1854 meeting. By year's end, five of the seven positions had been vacated. The board's viability, and consequently the seminary's, fell on the shoulders of its soon-to-be chairman, General George Mason Graham, a native Virginian. Graham, who came to Louisiana to manage his father's lands, knew the importance of higher education. He had attended West Point and the University of Virginia, though he graduated from neither. His well-balanced background helped Graham keep the other trustees focused as they struggled to open the seminary.

Seminary construction began in turmoil and went down hill from there. The designer, Alexander T. Wood, had died. John Reynolds became the resident architect. The contractor, Edward Crutchfield of Louisville, was slow and unreliable. Substandard materials, faulty workmanship, and poor supervision led to collapse of a tower, delaying completion for over a year. The board replaced Crutchfield and Reynolds with a competent architect, Alfred Freret of New Orleans.

In 1855, the General Assembly severely weakened the trustees by stripping them of many of their duties and leaving them in limbo. During its 1857 session, the assembly finished the job by creating a new Board of Visitors, which would supplement rather than replace the original Board of Trustees. The visitors, dominated by outsiders, would select the faculty and the curriculum while the trustees were to complete and maintain the building, then operate the school. Dual boards were widely used by New England colleges, such as Harvard, Bates, Brown, and Bowdin. This concept may have been popular in New England, but not in Rapides Parish, Louisiana.

The trustees felt insulted. Country folks might be able to erect a building, but not, it appeared, to run a college. Graham, named to the new board, refused to serve, then resigned in disgust from the old board as well. Meanwhile, the new Board of Visitors, primarily because of Graham's forceful objections, never met.

In 1858 the assembly tried to resolve its impasse with the trustees by instituting yet another board. This fourteen-member Board of Supervisors would not only select the faculty and operate the school, but, unlike the visitors, the supervisors were to assume complete control of the buildings once they were completed by the trustees. Aiding in the transition, Graham and Dr. Stokes A. Smith, the two presidents of the trustees, were named to the new board. It was this board which appointed William Tecumseh Sherman as the seminary's first superintendent.

Outgoing Governor Wickcliffe urged the incoming Assembly to pass legislation "fixing . . . the military character of the institution."

The General Assembly debated the bill at length before adopting an awkward compromise in March 1860, the Louisiana State Seminary of Learning and Military Academy. During the same session, the school was awarded an appropriation of $20,000—for the first time over and above the interest on the seminary fund.

Sherman found himself facing a change of governors with little continuity between the two administrations. From a philosophical standpoint, he related better to Wickcliffe. Yet he and Moore shared a strong mutual respect.

He may have lacked prior experience in higher education, but Sherman completed a credible first year as superintendent. Most of the cadets, 59 to be exact, satisfactorily completed their first work. When the second session opened on November 1, 1860, the seminary enrollment reached 80 on opening day. It rose to about 115 by the middle of the school year.

If Sherman thought the second year would be easier, he was wrong. A few days after classes began, Abraham Lincoln was elected president. The more moderate leaders in Louisiana wanted to wait to secede until after Lincoln's inauguration in March to get a better understanding of his program. Sherman enjoyed Louisiana, loved the school, and wanted to remain. But as he wrote to the governor, "If Louisiana withdraws from the Federal Union, I prefer to maintain my allegiance to the constitution as long as a fragment of it survives."

But Sherman did not wait for secession. In January 1861, Governor Moore ordered his new state militia to capture the arsenal in Baton Rouge. Once the seminary received captured arms marked "U.S.," Sherman notified the board that he was stepping down and turning the seminary's military command over to his commandant, Francis Smith.

By the end of January 1861, Louisiana had become the sixth state to secede. On February 9, the Board of Supervisors accepted Sherman's resignation to become effective February 28, but not before expressing its deep appreciation for his work. Similar expressions of gratitude came from his faculty, the governor, and several other state leaders. Some even suggested that Sherman, a moderate on the slavery issue, might fight for the South.

On February 20, 1861, Sherman ordered his corps of cadets to the parade ground for the last time. As one account goes, he gave a short talk, then walked along the formation extending a personal farewell to each of the teary-eyed students. Turning to address the faculty, he broke down and cried, then quietly departed. Only fourteen months earlier, he had opened the seminary doors for the first time.

The seminary, the largest structure then remaining in Confederate Louisiana, is portrayed on the state's new $100 bill. Courtesy of the author.

Sherman doubted that war was imminent. So, apparently, did the United States Army, which expressed no immediate plans for Sherman's services. Back in Ohio and out of work, he accepted the presidency of a street railway company in St. Louis. Louisiana did not forget Sherman and, even in such trying times, honored its obligations to him. On March 18, three days before Louisiana joined the Confederate States of America, Governor Moore signed an appropriations bill that included $500 due Sherman in back pay.

Within weeks, most cadets old enough to serve had left school to enlist in the Confederate Army, even Louis E. Woods, who left the seminary earlier to attend West Point. Many, such as Captain George W. Stafford, used their seminary training in military drills to become officers while still in their teens. Only one, Henry Taliaferro, joined the Union forces. Those still around on June 30, when the session ended, followed Professor Boyd to Camp Moore to serve under General Richard Taylor.

1857	1858	1859	1860
A board of visitors is created by the Assembly to augment rather than replace the board of trustees. Dual-board concept popular in New England but not in Rapides Parish, Louisiana.	Board of supervisors is created to eliminate the impasse between the dual boards. Governor becomes the ex officio chairman and Graham the vice-chairman.	Board of supervisors selects the superintendent, retired major William Tecumseh Sherman, and the seminary's first four faculty members.	Classes begin at the seminary. Nineteen students show up on opening day. Others follow.

2   Surviving the War

The Civil War ravaged southern colleges as well as other areas of life. A shortage of teachers, students, texts, material, and money combined to leave higher education in disarray. Almost all southern schools closed down; the seminary was no exception.

The board declined to promote Sherman's choice to replace him, Commandant Francis Smith. It looked instead to two recently resigned army officers—first to Colonel George W. Lay, then to Captain William R. Boggs. Each was willing to serve, but opted instead to join the Confederate Army. On May 14 the three Virginians on the faculty—Professors Smith, Clarke, and Boyd—resigned from the seminary. Boyd agreed to remain through the end of June and the school year.

Board members had to rely on Professors Vallas and St. Ange to begin the 1861–62 academic year. The patriotic fervor sweeping the state left few young men in school. When the seminary missed its scheduled November 1 starting date, many, including most board members, wondered if it would ever open again.

An artillery battery drills in front of the Pentagon Barracks on old campus. Photograph by Andrew Lytle.

1861

Louisiana leaves the Union, first as an independent nation, then as a member of the Confederacy. Sherman resigns.

Prodded by the General Assembly, the seminary commenced its third session but not until April 1, 1862. Dr. Vallas implemented a faculty decision of June 1861 to add a sub-freshman class and dropped the minimum age to fourteen to accommodate them. Though his changes weakened the school scholastically, they were necessary for the seminary's continuance. Of the thirty-nine students enrolling, all but nine were sub-freshmen.

Once the session was under way, Vallas, an Episcopal priest, was replaced as superintendent by another clergyman, Reverend W. E. M. Littlefield, a Methodist minister. St. Ange, formerly a French marine officer, remained as commandant. William A. Seay, an experienced Shreveport attorney, arrived to round out the faculty.

The Confederacy recruited large numbers of troops in Louisiana but transferred most for action elsewhere. This left the strategic lower Mississippi Valley, along with southern and central Louisiana, very vulnerable. Days after the seminary's third session began, New Orleans fell easily to the Union navy, prompting Governor Moore to relocate the state capital to Opelousas and, a short time later, to Shreveport. Maintaining contact with the peripatetic state administration proved to be a real challenge.

This third session was successful, though brief. Much of the work performed by the fifth classmen was remedial. And the students were younger—only three were over eighteen. The seminary persuaded President Jefferson Davis to exempt these three from conscription since, as cadet officers, their presence was necessary for an effective military organization. Davis, however, denied a blanket exemption for future students over eighteen.

The fourth session began on November 1, 1862, with 112 students, but most were young and ill prepared to study. They began to grow restless. Around the first of April, as Union troops approached Alexandria, the weary cadets mutinied, destroyed furniture, and forced Littlefield to quit. Seay, named acting superintendent, kept the school together until April 23, 1863, when the session ended and school closed for the duration.

The board, having qualms about its staffing, had already decided to reorganize under the leadership of two former professors, both Confederate majors sta-

David French Boyd

tioned in Virginia. One was Francis W. Smith, previously recommended for the post by Sherman but snubbed by the board. The other was David Boyd.

Once Smith and Boyd were approached by the board, the two met on the Virginia front lines to draft a comprehensive plan of reorganization. Smith declined to leave the service at that time. Boyd was able to resign his commission and return to Louisiana and the seminary.

In May 1863, Union general Nathaniel P. Banks briefly occupied Alexandria and the seminary. By the time Boyd reached the campus, Banks had removed his troops to Port Hudson to assist with the siege there. With neither faculty nor students, and no way to reopen the school any time soon, Boyd reenlisted. The board then released the campus buildings to General E. Kirby Smith for a Confederate army hospital.

Fighting in the area continued; two nearby battles heavily impacted the future of the entire Confederacy. Vicksburg fell on July 4 (as did Gettysburg in the east) and Port Hudson five days later. These rebel losses gave federal troops virtual control of the Mississippi River.

1862

Morrill Act is signed, authorizing the United States to issue land grants to states and territories that agree (all did) to establish a college to teach agriculture and the mechanical arts.

At the outbreak of the Civil War, these cannons (pictured in the foreground) fired on Fort Sumter, South Carolina, according to legend. After the war, Sherman supposedly presented them to LSU president David Boyd. These weapons stood in front of the president's home on the old campus and are now located in front of the Military and Air Science Building. Photograph by Andrew Lytle.

A weakened Trans-Mississippi Department, meant to protect Alexandria and the remaining Confederate areas west of the river, now faced a new enemy. They were the jayhawkers, gangs of draft dodgers, thieves, deserters, and thugs preying primarily on unprotected civilians.

Early in 1864, a band of these jayhawkers captured Boyd, then a Confederate officer, and took him to Natchez, where they sold him to the Union forces . The timing and the location was fortuitous for Boyd. Sherman, his old mentor and now a Union general, would be in nearby Vicksburg within days. Boyd wrote to ask if Sherman would transfer him to New Orleans, where his chances of parole would be better since Banks and Confederate general Richard Taylor frequently exchanged prisoners. Sherman not only agreed, but while en route to New Orleans on the steamer *Diana,* stopped at Natchez to pick up his prisoner of war. Once on board, Boyd had a tearful reunion with his old colleague. After bidding Sherman farewell, Boyd wrote, "altho' we are public enemies, we must always be private friends." Boyd remained a prisoner in New Orleans longer than he expected but was released in June during a prisoner exchange.

During the spring of 1864, Union forces embarked on the Red River campaign—Admiral David Porter by river and General Banks by land. Both were repulsed before reaching their objective of Shreveport. Banks became bitter in defeat. During their retreat from Sabine Cross Roads, his troops stopped in Alexandria long enough to plunder and torch the unprotected

community. Banks destroyed George Mason Graham's plantation across the river but left the seminary intact.

By that time Louisiana had two civil governments—the Confederate one still domiciled in Shreveport and the one supported by Union forces based in New Orleans. Henry Watkins Allen was the Confederate governor. His Union counterpart was Michael Hahn, whose lieutenant governor, James Madison Wells, was a staunch Unionist from Rapides Parish.

In March 1865, after Hahn was elected (but never seated) as a U.S. senator, Lieutenant Governor Wells became governor. As April progressed, the Confederacy collapsed at a dizzying speed. In quick order, the capital at Richmond fell, President Abraham Lincoln was assassinated, Robert E. Lee surrendered to Ulysses S. Grant at Appomattox, and Albert Sidney Johnston capitulated to Sherman in the east.

In early May, President Jefferson Davis was captured in Georgia on his way to the Trans-Mississippi Department, where he hoped to regroup. Instead, he was shackled and imprisoned. Later that month, General E. Kirby Smith, out of options, surrendered his department, the last major Confederate command to fall. After the state capital in Shreveport shut down, the seminary faced the disheartening prospect of dealing with a new Union administration in New Orleans. Within days, the remaining Confederate armies disbanded. War over and resistance gone, the Union forces quickly moved in to occupy the entire state, including Alexandria and the seminary property.

Boyd planned to reopen the seminary with Major Francis W. Smith's help, but Smith was killed in action during the waning days of the war. This left it to Boyd alone to get the seminary up and running again. Fortunately the local Union commanders, including the volatile George Armstrong Custer, proved to be cooperative.

From a distance, the seminary still looked impressive even after the war. Actually, the building was seriously in need of repair. Furniture was destroyed, scientific equipment was missing, roofs were leaking, and

Cadets practice their marksmanship in a drill. Photograph by Andrew Lytle.

floors were rotting. Much of the blame has been placed on the Union forces, who were indeed partially responsible. The jayhawkers probably did most of the damage. The Confederate troops certainly did their share. And then there were the nearby residents, who never hesitated to "borrow" needed furniture. Boyd faced an uphill battle, to say the least. He no longer had facilities; the seminary, although in disrepair, was still being used as a U.S. army hospital. He no longer had a board; all terms had lapsed without replacements having been named. He no longer had an easy-to-approach governor; Moore and Allen had escaped to Mexico to avoid arrest as political prisoners. He no longer had Francis

Smith to assist him. And he may not have had the necessary educational background to head the school. It was assumed at the time that he held a Master of Arts degree from the University of Virginia, but biographer Germaine M. Reed found that although he attended he did not graduate.

Boyd's task, at least on paper, looked impossible. But that was before one factored in the intangibles. Boyd had the perseverance, the determination, the vision, and above all, he soon had George Mason Graham back on the Board of Supervisors. The coming years would prove that David Boyd would make many personal sacrifices to keep the seminary alive.

Early cadets of the "Ole War Skule." Photograph by Andrew Lytle.

1863

The seminary closes for the duration as Union forces approach the campus. Troops leave after a brief stay, allowing the seminary to be used as a Confederate army hospital.

1864

Union forces embark on their Red River Campaign through the area in hopes of capturing the state capital at Shreveport. Repelled at Sabine Cross Roads, the retreating bluecoats ransack Alexandria but not the seminary.

3   LSU and Reconstruction

Superintendent Boyd reopened the seminary in October 1865. Only four students showed up on opening day. Before registration was over, there were sixty-six preparatory students and thirty-two freshmen.

The key to Boyd's success in the next four years would be his tenacity through four state administrations. The first of these governors was James Madison Wells from Rapides Parish. Essentially the only candidate in the 1865 gubernatorial race, Wells won handily statewide although trampled by a write-in aspirant in his home parish.

The governor, by law, was the board's ex-officio chairman. Graham resumed his earlier role as vice-chairman until he later stepped down in favor of his neighbor, W. T. Sanford. Boyd was named superintendent.

Wells, though a Unionist, never wavered in his support of the seminary. He even arranged for it to

Members of this rifle company and a few "civilians" take a break, ca. 1898. Photograph from the Alvin E. Rabenhorst Photograph Collection.

Staff under the Commandant of Cadets

borrow money against its annuity so it could begin repairs before classes started. He also led the fight to increase funding, making the school one of the strongest in the postwar South.

A civilian governor elected by the voters, Wells was nevertheless removed from office by the army in June 1867. He was superseded by a military governor, Benjamin Flanders, and a few months later by another, Joshua Baker. Baker served until 1868 when carpetbagger Henry Clay Warmoth, an Illinoisan still in his twenties, assumed office.

Boyd worked well with all four governors but occasionally rankled lawmakers. For example, he was accused of hiring too many former Confederate officers for faculty members, especially angering Unionists with the addition of a popular Rebel admiral, Raphael Semmes, in 1866. This tension was relieved when Semmes resigned.

Boyd invited Sherman to speak at the 1869 commencement ceremony. The general had a conflict on the June date but readily agreed to visit in February. Inviting the general was a gutsy move. Considering the strong anti-Union feelings of some Louisianians, such a visit presented a risk to both Sherman and the seminary. Yet Sherman's stay turned into a public relations plum for Boyd and the school. Alexandria's *Louisiana Democrat* hoped that its readers, "while they may not forget the bloody scenes of the war, [would be] willing to 'let the dead bury the dead,' [and] treat him with respect and kindness."

Sherman arrived with his daughter and went immediately to his room in the Ice House Hotel, where he received the townspeople and renewed friendships. The following day, Sherman rode out to the campus, seeing it for the first time since his emotional farewell eight years before. Whatever apprehension the newspaper and others may have had, they had no cause for concern. The general departed Alexandria on Wednesday, having been well received.

Other good things happened to the seminary.

Thanks to the General Assembly, the seminary received funding for a number of items close to Boyd's heart—new faculty homes, laboratory equipment, library books, a statewide topographical and geographical survey, and a good carriage road from the seminary to Alexandria, about three and a half miles away. Personal good news came to Boyd when his wife, Esther, gave birth to twins in April.

The highlight of the seminary's Reconstruction years came at the June 1869 commencement. No matter that only eight graduated, it was a milestone for Louisiana—one that brought in throngs of participants. The degrees were the first ever conferred on the Rapides Parish campus.

At high noon, to the sound of a bugle, the cadets marched into the chapel. Following the preliminary orations and essays, Boyd rose and delivered the baccalaureate address. Then the seminary's patron saint, George Mason Graham, presented diplomas to these first graduates, sending them out into an uncertain world to the music of a brass band. After breaking an hour for lunch, the cadets and guests returned for the commencement address by Henry M. Spofford, a former justice of the state supreme court, who tackled the subject of "veracity" and the lack of sincerity in both church and state affairs. As evening approached, seriousness faded into merriment. Cadets and their ladies attended a "hop," dancing until dawn. After a few hours of rest, they boarded the steamer *Celeste* for an overnight trip to the mouth of Cane River and back.

Boyd and his supporters had no way of knowing this first commencement at Rapides Parish would also be the last. Politics and various disasters were about to intervene.

The 1864 Louisiana Constitution had been acclaimed by Abraham Lincoln. Once the president died, however, it was rejected by the Radicals in Congress, who insisted on a new, more restrictive instrument. The constitutional convention met at New Orleans late in 1867 with ninety-eight delegates, forty-nine blacks and forty-nine whites, all but two being Republicans.

Out-of-state Radicals, in spite of segregation in many northern schools, demanded immediate mixing of races in all Louisiana institutions. Boyd did not oppose education for blacks but felt that instant desegregation of the seminary would alienate sufficient law-makers to curtail funding, causing all students to lose out. He felt that Louisiana's black and white leaders could develop a workable plan without outside help.

After many discussions and several drafts of the constitution, the final article regarding desegregation was worded vaguely enough to allow deal making. Leaders forged a compromise providing blacks and whites with what they wanted. They left the State Seminary alone while initiating comparable funding to private black colleges, including Straight University in New Orleans. The remaining problems revolved around money and competition. The assembly provided more for state cadets than ever before, disbursing $400 per year for each, compared to $410 paid annually by regular students. However, regular cadets were forced to pay in U.S. currency while the state paid for its cadets in treasury warrants, basically IOUs issued by the state. When the seminary bought goods, supplies, books, and just about everything else, merchants wanting cash would discount the warrants received at the going rate—up to seventy cents on a dollar. So in effect, the more money the seminary acquired from the state in the form of warrants, the more money it lost.

In late 1868, Boyd acknowledged to the General Assembly that the lack of fire-fighting equipment left the seminary vulnerable to fire, but then he let the matter drop. Although fire destroyed Spring Hill College near Mobile, Alabama, in February 1869, forcing a temporary relocation to St. Charles College, an academy near Grand Couteau in St. Landry Parish, it failed to stir Boyd to action on the need for fire protection. His greatest concern at the moment was the depreciated warrants from the state, which were already keeping the seminary from meeting its obligations.

In October 1869, David Boyd was confronted with two crises. Early that month, George Mason Graham had a serious accident, receiving injuries from which he would never fully recover. Then, at 2:00 A.M. on October 15, just three and one-half months after the successful commencement, the commissary caught on fire. Students, faculty, and staff pitched in to fight it, only to find the wooden floors and wall furring turning into an inferno. Lacking the necessary water and equipment, they could no nothing effective as the blaze roared out of control. By 4:00 A.M., the west wing collapsed. It was a gut-wrenching sight. The cadets' dream

1865

Federal troops use the seminary as a hospital. David Boyd reopens the seminary as its president. Graham again heads the board of supervisors.

of a college education seemed to be going up in flames along with their personal belongings. As the building was being destroyed, they tried to save what might be salvaged—the furniture, library books, and lab equipment.

The cause remained unknown. No matter what started the fire, the result was total loss of the building. Alexandria civic leaders found temporary quarters for the 133 remaining cadets in the Ice House Hotel until arrangements could be made for them to return home and await further instructions.

Boyd assumed full responsibility for not having prepared for fire, but did not allow himself to dwell on it. Time was now critical. He had to move quickly, even before conferring with his board.

On November 1, 1869, just a few days after its disastrous fire, the seminary reopened at Baton Rouge in the north wing of the State Institution for the Deaf and Dumb and the Blind. The move bordered on the miraculous. In addition to logistical challenges, the seminary faced an unwilling landlord. The structure was far from full, but asylum officials, fearing the loss of their building to interlopers, had no desire to share it. Governor Warmoth twisted arms—with results. In spite of their hostility, the asylum officials let the seminary move in.

The seminary, with its "temporary" relocation to Baton Rouge, reported a net gain of seven students, losing only two while picking up nine. Only one professor declined to leave Alexandria. For the cadets, the move represented a fresh start in a far more inviting locale than the piney woods of Rapides Parish. Even better, in early 1870 the General Assembly gave the Louisiana State Seminary of Learning and Military Academy a new and more fitting name, *the* Louisiana State University.

Governance turned out to be awkward. Boyd ran the school on a day-to-day basis, but his board remained domiciled in Rapides Parish. His only direct contact with the board was through members of its three-man executive committee—usually Graham, Sanford (the new chairman), and one other—who made regular trips from Alexandria to Baton Rouge to review administrative matters. With its proximity to New Orleans, again the capital, LSU attracted far more legislative scrutiny.

Boyd felt comfortable negotiating with native white Louisiana lawmakers, especially those understanding the school and its goals. But these members, the Democrats, were now in a distinct minority. Like it or not, LSU now had to deal primarily with out-of-staters—carpetbaggers, former Union soldiers, anti-South zealots, malcontents, and the like. Joined by scalawags and blacks, they became the backbone of the

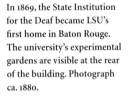

In 1869, the State Institution for the Deaf became LSU's first home in Baton Rouge. The university's experimental gardens are visible at the rear of the building. Photograph ca. 1880.

state's ruling Radical Republican Party. The New Orleans Custom House Ring, headed by James F. Casey, pulled this diverse group together as a political entity. No ordinary collector of customs, Casey was also President U. S. Grant's brother-in-law. In addition to controlling federal patronage, the Ring could call upon the attorney general in Washington, the army, and even the president for support. And it frequently did.

Confronting this new leadership in the General Assembly posed problems for Boyd, and he had to handle several unfortunate episodes. One involved an official visit to the campus by black legislators, with whom LSU's white commandant of cadets refused to shake hands. Another concerned Boyd's poor handling of a Radical Republican's job application. Fortunately LSU had a strong ally in Governor Henry Clay Warmoth. As long as he stayed in office, the school seemed immune to excessive legislative meddling.

Then there was the desegregation issue. New Orleans public schools, under the wing of Union troops, were as integrated as any in the nation. A private black university, Straight, now received state aid, and the Radicals, in turn, acquiesced to an all-white LSU, at least for a while. The governor appointed a black state representative, Henry Lott, an Alexandria barber, to the Board of Supervisors, and then to the executive committee. Otherwise, Warmoth generally left Boyd and LSU alone unless they asked for help.

The first of two elected carpetbag governors, Warmoth had become a lawyer at age eighteen, a Union army colonel at twenty, and Louisiana's chief executive at twenty-six. His success as governor stemmed from his ability to empathize with white Louisianians and their needs. As for LSU, in spite of his hectic schedule, Warmoth still found time to visit the campus.

The 1872 election was especially bewildering and corrupt. In the final analysis, William Pitt Kellogg became the new governor because President Grant wanted it that way. And his vote ended up being the only vote that really counted. Warmoth was out, never again to be a factor in Louisiana politics. Without him, officials at LSU were not sure what to expect.

William Pitt Kellogg, the state's second carpetbag governor, was an Illinois attorney who had been appointed by his friend, Abraham Lincoln, to serve as chief justice of the Nebraska Territory before arriving in New Orleans to head the Custom House. He served as a U.S. senator from 1868 until 1872.

When the new governor took office in 1873, LSU's student body consisted of 118 students, almost all beneficiary cadets, and a dozen or so professors—but not for long.

LSU had been paying its obligations with state treasury warrants, redeemable at par as the state collected sufficient income to pay them off. Through the late 1870s, the cash value of the warrants stayed close to seventy to seventy-five cents on a dollar. In anticipation of a rising market, Boyd arranged to borrow against the warrants, using the proceeds to pay off creditors in currency. But his plan backfired. The Democrats and the Radicals shared an uncanny knack of overspending the public's money, further depleting the state treasury and, in turn, impeding Louisiana's ability to redeem its warrants. The market value of state warrants, instead of rising, plummeted to fifty cents on a dollar. The reduced collateral not only subjected LSU to an immediate call of its loans, but pushed it to the brink of bankruptcy.

LSU received a small part of its income from those few students paying full tuition in U.S. currency. But most of its funding still came from the $350 in state warrants received for each beneficiary cadet. That amount at one time covered a student's entire needs other than clothing. By the 1872–73 school year, the value of the warrants had so deteriorated that the state's allocation covered tuition and board alone. In 1873 the assembly cut all funds to the beneficiary cadet program. By March, Boyd's only alternative was to furlough all of the state-subsidized cadets, virtually wiping out the student body. Next to go were the professors he could no longer pay. Enrollment declined to thirty-five in 1873–74 and to single-digit numbers the following year. The faculty bottomed out at two members, David and his younger brother Thomas, who had recently graduated at the top of LSU's class of 1872.

David Boyd toyed with the idea of launching an endowment fund underwritten with prepaid tuition. The university fortunately had another, though limited, source of income, for at least another year—the annual interest generated from the seminary bonds. But there were problems.

A constitutional amendment ratified in 1870 had restricted the state's bonded indebtedness to $25 million, an amount far exceeded by the free-wheeling Warmoth assembly. Governor Kellogg initiated extreme measures to stem the tide, reducing expenses and indebtedness. During early 1874, he pushed through the highly controversial Funding Act, which scaled down existing debt. New $600 consolidated or "consol" bonds yielding 7 percent and maturing in 1914 were issued to replace each of the state's outstanding $1,000 bonds, regardless of maturity or interest rate.

LSU had been receiving 6 percent interest on its $138,000 in seminary bonds, or $8,280 each year. These bonds were to be surrendered for new consol bonds, which would result in a 30 percent loss in annual income along with a 40 percent reduction in principal. Since funding for the seminary bonds had come from Congressional legislation, the supervisors took the position that the state's move was illegal. Thus they balked, refusing to submit their bonds for exchange for the new consols. The administration retaliated, instantly freezing all interest payments to the school.

Though heavily criticized, Kellogg's Funding Act of 1874 may well have saved Louisiana, and consequently LSU, from complete financial ruin. Yet for LSU to reap any long-term benefits, it first needed to withstand the short-term pressures. Its future looked bleak.

The seminary was initially established from a grant of 46,080 acres of public land from Washington. When it opened in 1860, a grateful seminary had expressed its appreciation and loyalty with this inscription over the front door: The Union *Esto Perpetua*. Within thirteen months, Louisiana had seceded from the Union and off came the inscription.

Now Boyd and the new LSU board returned, hat in hand, to request another federal land grant, one that would be dispensed under the 1862 Morrill Act. With its deserted classrooms and depleted bank accounts, the survival of LSU hinged on somehow tapping these new land-grant revenues. The state's primary institution of higher learning could continue only with the additional funding. Logic and necessity were on LSU's side. Politics and time were not.

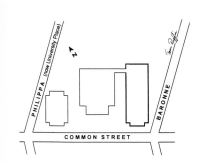

The Louisiana A&M College occupied the East Building of the University of Louisiana complex from 1874 until its merger with LSU in 1877. This three-building unit later became Tulane University's first campus. Courtesy Historic New Orleans Collection.

4 Morrill Land Grants

By the time the Civil War ended, American higher education was undergoing a metamorphosis. There had long been a dichotomy in educational opportunities. The children of America's elite could easily attend college. But the children of farmers and laborers—the bulk of the population—had few chances to further their learning. They needed new and affordable alternatives to the traditional classical studies. This difficult task was solved by Justin Smith Morrill.

Morrill's formal education ended when he was fourteen. The son of a blacksmith, he found outside work to help support his family. He eventually became a prominent merchant and farmer. By the time he reached his mid-forties, however, he sold his businesses to pursue a new career, that of a congressman. He championed the cause of higher education in Congress until his death in 1898.

Congressman Morrill appreciated the need for greater accessibility to higher education and for innovative new programs, those meeting the growing demands of agriculture, transportation, and industry. He introduced two bills to further common people's access to education. The first failed, but the second met with success.

On July 2, 1862, President Abraham Lincoln signed the Morrill Land-Grant Act into law, sparking a revolution in higher education. States suddenly found themselves opening and operating a new breed of college. The new schools offered a broader curriculum to far more students and became the vehicle by which the nation entered the technological age.

Few congressmen and senators realized the full thrust of Morrill's dream; the bill's passage came more through acquiescence than from overwhelming

Beyond the fields of LSU's horticulture garden, where the state capitol now stands, may be seen the buildings of the old campus. Photograph by Andrew Lytle.

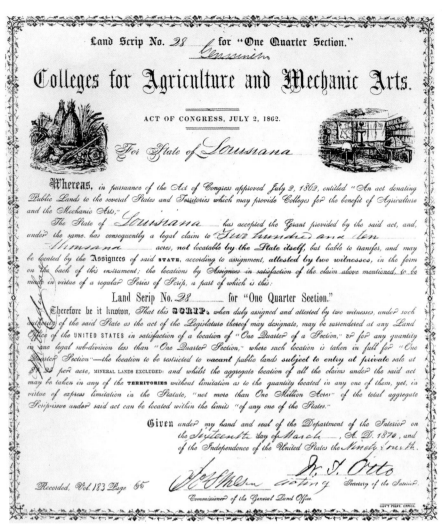

The reverse side was assigned in blank by John Lynch, assignor for the state, to be completed when resold by the land speculator. This particular scrip, number 28, was used by one Patrick Nevills to acquire a farm in Hall County, Nebraska. Source: National Archives

The United States helped fund the Louisiana A&M College by issuing to the state 1,312 scrip, each exchangeable for 160 acres of public lands in territories or other states. After selling the scrip in a single lot to a land speculator, Louisiana agreed to buy bonds with the proceeds, then use the interest to defray college operating expenses. Source: National Archives

support. Yet this legislation became the hallmark bill in higher education, since equaled in impact only by the GI Bill of 1944.

Apprenticeship continued to be the primary means of training professionals as well as skilled laborers during the early 1800s. Some aspiring professionals sought formal instruction that was more specialized than the conventional liberal arts curriculum. Scores of colleges responded with such new departments as medicine, law, and pharmacy. Most granted degrees after a single year of study with no prior college required. The University of Louisiana at New Orleans (chartered 1845) fit this pattern, although it supposedly offered an undergraduate degree as well.

Teacher education advanced significantly in 1839 when Massachusetts established its State Normal School, the nation's first. Others followed. Still two groups, considered trades rather than professions by many, continued to struggle—engineers and farmers.

The need for civil engineers emerged early with the designing of railroad rights-of-way, canals, and bridges. Steamboats, factories, and locomotives brought on a similar demand for mechanical engineers. The United States Military Academy, which opened in 1802, established the nation's first engineering curriculum. Civilian colleges, notably Rensselaer and Norwich, soon followed suit. The first major breakthrough came in 1847 when Harvard and Yale established new scientific schools. Later, when retired army officers became available for teaching, other colleges, including the Louisiana State Seminary, began offering civil engineering courses. Study in other engineering fields continued to lag behind.

Agriculture, the nation's leading industry, likewise suffered. Few farmers listened as Edmund Ruffin and other reformers promoted crop rotation, better fertilization, and other scientific techniques. Father-to-son training perpetuated outdated methods of past generations. To meet the challenge, Michigan and Maryland launched agricultural colleges, Pennsylvania opened a Farmers' High School, and Iowa had its State College and Farm. The Farmers' College in Ohio was among the few private institutions in the field.

The strong farm lobby pushed hard for more agricultural colleges. Their efforts evolved into a crusade to provide industrial universities to serve all of the industrial classes—mechanics and artisans in addition to farmers. This broader based support ultimately carried the day.

Following the Civil War, the South's education system was in shambles. The federal government's Reconstruction policies, many punitive in nature, hindered efforts for recovery. LSU and the other southern colleges struggled just to keep their doors open. Morrill's legislation was slow to help. Southern states were prohibited from participating as long as they remained "in condition of rebellion or insurrection."

To implement the Morrill Act, the cash-starved nation depended on land grants to schools as it had in the past and would continue to do in the future. The Morrill Act decreed that states were to receive 30,000 acres of federal land per each of their congressmen and senators. This meant Louisiana was entitled to 210,000 acres. States still having suitable U.S. public lands within their borders received actual acreage in place. The remaining states received scrip, which could be exchanged for unappropriated federal lands in other public-land states or territories.

States receiving scrip were severely handicapped. Prohibited by the act from owning land in other states, they were under financial pressure to sell to the only large buyers around, land speculators. The in-place states, in contrast, were able to select lands within their borders, hold them without paying taxes, trade up on a two-for-one basis for acreage adjacent to railroads, and

Commandant of Cadets' house on old campus. Photograph by Andrew Lytle.

generate income through leasing while waiting to sell. Louisiana actually had available federal public lands within its borders, but was precluded from using them by the Southern Homestead Act of 1866. The act, designed primarily to assist freedmen in homesteading, met with such limited success that it was repealed ten years later. Yet it forced Louisiana to go the less desirable "scrip" route.

Each state, in accepting the land grants, agreed to establish and operate at least one college teaching military science, agriculture, and the mechanical arts without excluding other scientific or classical studies. They also agreed to establish the school by July 1, 1874. Embracing the primary goal of promoting "liberal and practical education to the industrial classes," all existing (as well as later) states and territories accepted the offer, further consenting to placing all revenue into a perpetual fund, with 90 percent of the annual interest set aside for operating expenses. The remaining 10 per-

cent could be used for land acquisition but not for buildings.

By spurning pressure to standardize, the states developed their own institutions based on local needs and available resources. In the northeast, where high school graduates were common, colleges screened prospective students. The University of California (at Berkeley), closer to the norm, accepted "any resident of the age of fourteen, or upwards, of approved moral character." Many welcomed women; others did not.

The curriculums also varied. The leading farmers' organization, the Grange, exerted constant pressure, demanding new and better farming programs. Yet at least two land grant institutions never taught agriculture. The prescribed program in military tactics also ran into early snags when the army could not provide the necessary personnel at all schools.

Educators disputed the definition of mechanic arts. Detractors contended this referred strictly to voca-

1869

The seminary holds its first graduation, issuing eight degrees. Seminary burns to ground, forcing a "temporary" move to Baton Rouge, where it shares facilities with the State Institution for the Deaf and Dumb and the Blind.

tional courses—blacksmithing, carpentry, and the like. Land-grant educators insisted that this terminology encompassed all fields of engineering, including the emerging mechanical and electrical categories. Some even extended this to include mining.

In the end, Morrill's program provided seed money for institutions such as Pennsylvania State, Ohio State, Purdue, Cornell, Auburn, Texas A&M, and the Universities of California (at Berkeley), Illinois, and Florida, just to name a handful.

David Boyd avidly followed the land-grant movement. From the time he reopened the Rapides Parish campus, Boyd touted the State Seminary as the logical recipient. After all, his institution had the facilities with the needed infrastructure already in place. Good farm land was available close by. The seminary already taught a course in civil engineering. And it had a strong military heritage in place.

The General Assembly officially accepted the land

grant in March 1869. To obtain the scrip and negotiate its sales, the assembly also named a commission—the governor, the chief justice, and a third member appointed by the other two, John Lynch. But in October 1869, the State Seminary lost its edge by burning to the ground, necessitating a quick move to Baton Rouge. This fire and the move changed the odds.

April 8, 1871, was just another work day. When John Lynch reached his office that Saturday, he faced a large stack of forms to be completed and signed. They were land scrip, numbered one through 1,312, each exchangeable for a quarter section (180 acres) of unclaimed federal lands in other states or territories, for a total of 209,920 acres worth eighty-seven cents each when the scrip forms were signed and delivered to a land speculation firm in New York

These 1,312 sheets of paper provided the financial foundation for the A&M College and ultimately LSU.

The front side of each scrip had been signed earlier by the authorities in Washington certifying that Louisiana had access to certain acreage that it could assign to others. Lynch signed the reverse side on behalf of the state and delivered them to a land speculation firm in New York, which then sold one to each of 1,312 settlers.

The state received $182,630.40 to be invested in "safe stock," i.e., bonds, yielding 5 percent. Lynch did even better, purchasing depressed state bonds at a deep discount to reap more than $17,000 in annual interest. By the time the 1873 legislative session convened, reinvestment of interest had increased the face value of the bonds to $327,000 and the annual income to $19,620. As this figure grew, so did the competition for the Morrill grant. Boyd now reconciled himself to dividing the grant, as Lynch suggested, between LSU and all-black Straight University.

Then came a devastating blow. As Boyd fought for the Morrill revenue, he was blind-sided by the governor, who quit funding LSU's beneficiary cadet program.

Battle lines were quickly drawn for the 1874 legislative showdown. The top priority was to designate the

Baton Rouge volunteer fire companies display their equipment in front of the Pentagon Barracks.

1870

The seminary acquires a new name—the Louisiana State University.

1871

State entitled to 1312½ scrip exchangeable for 210,000 acres of U. S. public lands but lost 80 of those acres when federal government declined to issue a half-scrip.

Cadets drill for a crowd of spectators in these 1895 Andrew Lytle photographs. The Pentagon Barracks are visible in the background.

state's land-grant institution. Although it was never enforced, by law the recipient had to be in operation by July 1. Otherwise the funds were subject to reversion to the federal government.

In his opening statement to the assembly, Governor Kellogg acknowledged the strong sentiment in favor of Louisiana State University. Then he scoffed at its heavy debt and its lack of "accommodation" since the 1869 fire.

Boyd took the initiative with a new proposal: Bring LSU and the University of Louisiana (in New Orleans) together as a single institution under the latter's charter. The new A&M College would also be included, permitting it and LSU to become the literary, scientific, and technical departments of the University of Louisiana and be located in Baton Rouge. The University of Louisiana's medical and law departments would remain in New Orleans. As for the necessary experimental farm, the Baton Rouge Board of Aldermen voted unanimously to purchase one hundred acres for the school's use.

Two opposing house bills were introduced—one to place the A&M college under LSU, and the other to place it under the University of Louisiana. On February 27, 1873, the House Education Committee announced that, after a study of the various bills, it strongly recommended establishing still another institution, the Louisiana State Agricultural and Mechanical College at New Orleans. Once again, Boyd's plans for LSU were thwarted.

5 The A&M College

On April 7, 1874, Governor Kellogg signed the bill establishing the Louisiana State Agricultural and Mechanical College, then appointed the college's first Board of Control. Its makeup covered the gamut from dedicated citizens to political hacks, black and white. The board focused on its goal of providing higher education for the "industrial classes," both black and white—at least for those living in the New Orleans area.

The act envisioned a college located in a "country parish." Until the board determined the site, the A&M College used the University of Louisiana's east building at the corner of Common and Baronne Streets in New Orleans.

The board named Dr. Thomas Nicholson, a physician, as the school's first president. With the initial faculty on hand, Nicholson rushed to open the college's 1874 summer session—ostensibly to beat a July 1 Congressional deadline, but more likely to silence LSU and others still eyeing the Morrill funds.

To expand his statewide support, Nicholson published the *Agricultural & Mechanical College Journal for the State of Louisiana.* In addition to plugging the school, the *College Journal* provided farming and

Faculty members and students in the School of Agriculture not only maintained an experimental farm on the old campus, they also raised and studied livestock, including the cows pictured at left. Photo by Andrew Lytle.

household tips, such as this remedy for smallpox inflammation—rub on a mixture of gasoline, gum camphor, pulverized sulphite of soda, and pure carbolic acid.

By the time the regular fall semester commenced on November 15, the college was better prepared and had very little competition. LSU, still in Baton Rouge but no longer receiving state aid, saw its enrollment approach zero. The University of Louisiana, with professional schools in law and medicine, had discontinued its academic department.

The new A&M president, James Lucius Cross, a graduate of the Virginia Military Institute, wanted to fill the void by establishing a strong school. He had a highly competent faculty but a weak student body. With a minimum age of twelve (later raised to fourteen), few approached college caliber. Of the sixty cadets enrolling that fall, twenty were soon dropped from the rolls while others were placed on probation. Even the better students had to be tutored. While Cross

hoped to develop a strong A&M curriculum in time, at first he focused on the practical needs of his students, training them to become mechanics and artisans. To meet the requirements of the Morrill Act, Cross adopted a military format with cadets marching to and from class.

On paper, the A&M College started off on a strong financial footing. But the new school encountered LSU's problems with state cadets, depreciated warrants, and the scaling down of its bonds. Where to teach became as important as what to teach. The school had a building designed explicitly for college use by architect James Dakin. While it was the ideal setting for an urban trade school, it was not suitable for agricultural training, which remained a top priority under the Morrill Act.

This prompted an immediate search for a college farm site. The Board of Control ultimately picked the Chalmette Battlefield, which was just beyond the city limits in the adjacent St. Bernard Parish. The area,

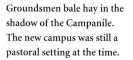

Groundsmen bale hay in the shadow of the Campanile. The new campus was still a pastoral setting at the time.

where Andrew Jackson won the 1815 Battle of New Orleans, was fertile, though badly neglected.

The land acquisition took place in 1875. The battlefield itself was owned by the State and thus available without cost. A nearby tract was bought for less than $1,600 from the City of New Orleans. The Board still needed the land connecting the first two parcels, whatever the price. And to many, that price paid was far too high: $20,555. The seller was none other than John Lynch's wife, Mary Atkins Lynch, in a transaction soon to haunt the school.

The A&M College now owned a 600-acre farm fronting on the Mississippi River. The board was ready to start erecting buildings, buying livestock, and teaching agriculture. It even talked of adding a training ship to teach the maritime trades. But Morrill bond interest could not be used for erecting farm structures. Although the assembly had previously appropriated $10,000 specifically for buildings, the state treasurer refused to issue the warrants for that amount. This forced the school to shelve plans for improving the Chalmette land. Adding to the insult, the General Assembly in 1875 established a joint committee to "investigate whether there is a bona fide Agricultural and Mechanical College."

Enrollment increased the next two years, but the college had yet to open its college farm at Chalmette, or to renovate its New Orleans building, which was badly in want of repair. The worst was still to come.

LSU—described by the A&M community as "the now bankrupt, destitute, and deserted institution, known in the past as the Louisiana State University"—still smarted over the loss of Morrill funds. Running short on both money and students, Superintendent Boyd had time on his hands. He used it to conceive a carefully orchestrated campaign to merge the A&M college into LSU.

First he needed an angle he could exploit. Remember the tract purchased from John Lynch's wife in 1875. David Boyd now accused Mrs. Lynch of having acquired the property the year before, then flipping it over to the A&M College for a quick profit in a tainted transaction. In reality, Mrs. Lynch had purchased the property for a homesite in January 1871—over four years before she sold it to the A&M College and over three years before the College was even created.

Cadets with their sponsor, ca. 1898. Each year, each company or battalion commander selected a sponsor, usually his sweetheart, for his unit. Photograph from the Alvin E. Rabenhorst Photograph Collection.

Relying on these flawed allegations, Boyd made his move during the 1876 session. Although expecting the Democrats to carry the bill, he shrewdly called on a white Republican friend of LSU to introduce it in the House. Caddo Parish's Aaron B. Levisee, and a black Republican friend, East Baton Rouge Parish's J. Henri Burch, were to lead the Senate battle. Boyd's groundwork paid off. In spite of strong opposition from the A&M board, the Grange, and the New Orleans press, the legislation was approved during the spring of 1876 by the General Assembly and sent to Governor Kellogg. The bill would unite the Louisiana State University . . . and the Agricultural and Mechanical College . . . into one and the same institution of learning, to be known and designated under the name and title of the Louisiana State University and Agriculture and Mechanical College."

That legislation should have written *finis* to the A&M College, but Governor William Pitt Kellogg neither signed nor vetoed it. Under the constitutional provisions of that day, the LSU people somehow had to retrieve the original bill, then wait until January 1, 1877, when the new legislature met, and have it promulgated (i.e., published in the official journal) by the secretary of state. Only then would it become law. Completing

1873

Over LSU's objections, state gives land-grant funds to the new Agricultural and Mechanical College, which opens on the University of Louisiana campus in New Orleans.

1874

The A&M Board acquires three lots at the Chalmette Battlefield for a college farm and their own campus.

In the late 1880s, university officials and faculty members lived in the Colony, located on the old campus. The building was later used as a dormitory.

these vital steps, it turned out, would be neither simple nor easy.

By January Louisianians had another governor; actually, to no one's surprise, they had two. One was Republican Stephen B. Packard and the other, Democrat Francis B. Nicholls, each professing victory based on their respective vote counts. David Boyd, working closely with State Senator J. Henri Burch, proceeded with Packard, the claimant backed by the Union troops and President Grant—and most likely to remain in office.

On January 23, 1877, Burch unearthed the original bill, then he and David Boyd presented it to Emile Honoré, Packard's secretary of state, requesting its promulgation. Once published in the official state journal, the New Orleans *Republican,* on January 31, the bill officially became Act 103 of 1876.

The 1876 presidential election was indeed close (far closer than the 2000 race). A single electoral vote determined the victor in a dispute lasting not five weeks,

but four months. Louisiana and two other southern states (yes, one was Florida) submitted two sets of returns. Democrat Samuel J. Tilden needed just one of the contested electoral votes to win; Republican Rutherford B. Hayes needed all. In the end, the decision came down to a series of informal agreements just before inauguration day between southern politicians, who wanted to rid the South of the occupation forces, and friends of Hayes, who wanted the presidency. On March 2, 1877, the electoral vote was finally counted—in favor of Hayes. Three days later he took the oath of office.

The end result placed Republican Hayes in the White House, Republican William Pitt Kellogg in the U.S. Senate, Democrat Francis T. Nicholls as Louisiana's governor, and the Democrats in control of the General Assembly. Furthermore, the federal troops went home, effectively ending Reconstruction in Louisiana. Left out in the cold were Packard, his legislature, and LSU.

1876

1877

General Assembly votes to merge the A&M College into LSU, but governor neither signs nor vetoes the bill, leaving its status in doubt.

Bill finally promulgated by each of two rival state administrations and becomes law. LSU absorbs the A&M College, and its land-grant status—and becomes the Louisiana State University and Agricultural and Mechanical College.

When Packard's administration collapsed, the validity of its actions, including the promulgation, came under attack. LSU had to start anew with Governor Nicholls, not known for his strong support of education.

This delay gave supporters of the A&M College a chance to regroup. They introduced one bill to investigate LSU, another to repeal the merger. The Grangers, when given seats on the new board, withdrew their opposition, allowing Nicholls's secretary of state to move ahead with promulgation—this time in the new official journal, the New Orleans *Daily Democrat,* on June 1, 1877. After a long but fruitful wait, the merger bill became law—but with a different number, Act 145 of 1876. On October 5, 1877, an all-white LSU opened in Baton Rouge under its new name—*the* Louisiana State University and Agricultural and Mechanical College—and in the process, became the state's land-grant college. Although still referred to as LSU or the LSU, it was a different school. Unexpectedly, its new designation would bring with it millions of dollars of future federal revenue.

As for the original A&M College, it returned its classroom building to University of Louisiana and surrendered its 600-acre college farm at Chalmette to LSU, then faded quietly into oblivion.

Stately oak trees lined the drive leading to the Pentagon Barracks on old campus. Photograph by Andrew Lytle.

6   LSU and the Bourbon Democrats

David Boyd reconsidered an earlier stand and accepted the presidency of the combined LSU. He looked forward to the political return of native white Democrats—the "Redeemers," as they called themselves, or Bourbon Democrats, as opponents called them—who tried to restore the antebellum power structure. But he soon found himself at greater odds with the new political leaders than the old. While the carpetbaggers had left the state, he quickly realized, corruption had remained behind.

The 1879 Constitution was a mixed blessing for LSU. Baton Rouge became the permanent home for both the state capital and LSU for the first time. The university now faced greater supervision from the legislature, but also could benefit from a closer relationship with the lawmakers.

LSU still had its land-grant revenue, though less than before. The Republicans' Funding Act of 1874 had already slashed the income from both of its land grants. Now the new constitution cut the total still further—to under $15,000 per year—but continued to give LSU a financial edge over the other state schools.

The 1880s developed into another tumultuous decade for LSU. Four different men, two of them twice, would serve as LSU president, and all would have trouble with the Board of Supervisors and the state administration.

Louis Alfred Wiltz, who became governor in 1880, insisted the new constitution gave him the authority to select an entirely new Board of Supervisors. David Boyd encountered resistance from the board, dissension within the faculty, clashes with the governor, and

Founded in 1893 by Cadet Captain W. M. Barrow and Cadet Lieutenant Ruffin G. Pleasant, LSU's band was a military band until World War II. In this 1914 photograph, band members take a break from performing to enjoy their boxed lunches. From the Jasper Ewing Collection.

Professor James W. Nicholson's math class on the old campus, ca. 1890s.

hostility from the General Assembly. That autumn brought with it an inevitable finale: Boyd was fired.

In October 1880, the LSU board named his replacement—William Preston Johnston, a Yale graduate then occupying a chair under General Robert E. Lee at Washington College (now Washington and Lee University). Johnston was the son of General Albert Sidney Johnston, a Confederate hero. The new LSU president had also been a Confederate officer, serving first in battle and afterwards on President Jefferson Davis's staff.

Johnston faced the same divided board and many of the same problems. The student body consisted of thirty-eight students when he arrived. The university offered only two four-year degrees (B.S. and B.A.) and two two-year certificates (in agriculture and engineering), but no degrees had been awarded during the previous seven years.

Johnston also faced problems in Chalmette. On Oc-

tober 1, 1881, St. Bernard Parish sheriff E. E. Nunez auctioned a farm recently seized at foreclosure. What was so unusual was not the foreclosure but the land involved; it was one of three parcels acquired in 1875 by Louisiana A&M College for their college farm and second campus (the Lynch property). Before developing the acreage, the school was forced to merge with LSU, which, strapped for cash, could not continue to make the mortgage payments. The Citizens Bank, as high bidder, acquired the river front property for a mere $6,770.

By 1882 Johnston appeared to be making progress. He began tackling farmers' demands for a stronger agricultural curriculum. When the university surgeon, J. W. Dupree, began to produce a badly needed smallpox vaccine, LSU made it available to residents of Louisiana and nearby states. Graduations resumed. Enrollment increased, but so did infighting among board

1881

LSU loses one of three parcels at Chalmette (the Lynch property) to foreclosure.

Pentagon Barracks on the old campus, ca. 1895. Photograph by Andrew Lytle.

members. Meanwhile, Johnston's position grew more precarious.

On January 16, 1883, Johnston received an offer from the Tulane Educational Fund to head its new university. Although the new school existed only on paper, he jumped at the opportunity. James W. Nicholson became LSU's next president. After serving in the Confederate army, he'd been president of a college in Claiborne Parish before joining LSU and attaining prominence as a mathematics professor. Nicholson tried to strengthen the scientific agricultural program despite continuing conflicts with the board. But after a year of problems with the board and faculty, Nicholson decided to step down and resume teaching, paving the way for David Boyd to return.

When James W. Nicholson resigned as LSU's president during the spring of 1884, David Boyd was serving as president of another land-grant school—the Agri-

culture and Mechanical College of Alabama (now Auburn University). But Boyd encountered greater problems there, because Alabama A&M faculty could veto Boyd's policy decisions. Boyd also suffered a catastrophic loss there: Two of his young sons accidentally shot another of his sons to death. At the end of the 1883–84 school year, when his old job at LSU opened, Boyd was ready to return to Baton Rouge.

Boyd found his homecoming to be as acrimonious as his departure. Faculty morale was still low, cadet discipline still weak, and the board still hostile. In addition to internal pressures, LSU, and consequently Boyd, faced external ones as well. Particularly troubling was the growing aggression of the Patrons of Husbandry, better known as the Grange. This broad-based farmers' association quickly prodded the stand-alone land-grant schools and their governing bodies toward emphasizing agriculture at the expense of other pro-

1884

LSU receives a restricted title to abandoned Baton Rouge Army Arsenal, consisting of Pentagon Barracks and a score of other buildings. The university moves in.

grams. The terms "cow college" and "silo tech" soon became widespread.

Within the A&M environment, it was the humanists who emerged as the Grangers' chief foe. The farmers distrusted the liberal arts professors, holding them responsible for farm children, once educated, having little desire to return to the farm. The Grange especially disliked schools like LSU, where the state university and the A&M college were combined. The farm organizations felt all land-grant schools were *their* schools, thereby insisting on a strong agricultural bias. Should their demands not be met, they would then press the colleges to divest their agricultural schools along with their Morrill grant funds.

This threat was real. Bowing to the farmers' demands during the 1880s, lawmakers in the Carolinas snatched land-grant funds away from their state universities and gave them to two upstart colleges—North Carolina A&M (now North Carolina State University) and Clemson. The Grange in Mississippi forced the legislature to strip the Morrill funds from the University of Mississippi and gave them to the new Missis-

sippi A&M (now Mississippi State). At LSU, board member Robert H. Ryland, master of the Grange and a member of the old A&M College board, led the fight to separate the agricultural school from the university.

Boyd agreed that LSU's agricultural offerings were weak. He enticed Dr. William C. Stubbs, one of his top professors at Alabama A&M, to develop a crash agricultural program at LSU. In his new role, Stubbs split his duties between teaching at LSU and directing the state's first experiment station, recently opened by the Sugar Planters Association in Kenner, but soon moved to Audubon Park (between Magazine Street and the river). The farmers' tongue-lashing turned to praise.

Improving the agricultural program would soon pay off for LSU. A resurgence of farmer interest in more practical education goaded Congress into passing the 1887 Hatch Act—which allotted $15,000 annually to each state to fund agricultural experiment stations. Louisiana had a head start, already having one station at Audubon Park and two more on the way. A later station even evolved into the site for the Alexandria campus.

These engineering students hone their skills in a workshop on the old campus, ca. 1897.

Mechanical drawing class, Robertson Hall, old campus, 1897.

Boyd's next challenge was finding a permanent home for LSU. In 1870 Boyd had first contacted his old friend Sherman, who was commanding general of the U.S. army at the time, to discuss the ideal spot, the abandoned army post near downtown Baton Rouge. This was the site of the Baton Rouge Arsenal that the Louisiana Militia had captured in early 1861, causing Sherman to resign from his post as LSU's first superintendent. The arsenal was reoccupied by federal troops during the Civil War and until the end of Reconstruction.

Sherman originally rejected the idea of transferring the arsenal to the school, feeling the post might be needed by the army at some later date. Following a visit to LSU in 1879, he reversed his position. But no decision would be reached for a few more years.

When Boyd returned to LSU in 1884, he resumed this discussion. By this time, the property had been transferred from the War Department to the Interior Department. Negotiations proceeded smoothly, and in September 1886, Congress conveyed the garrison lands to LSU, subject to restrictions.

The new campus, in contrast to the crowded facility it replaced, contained slightly over 200 acres. It stretched from the river eastward to Plank Road, encompassing enough land for an on-campus horticultural garden and an experimental farm. The center of activity was an impressive four-building complex in a five-sided layout. The open side, where a fifth building once stood, faced the river. Known as the Pentagon or Quintagonal Barracks, the structures still stand, now in the shadows of the present state capitol. Across the unpaved drive, an extension of Third Street, was the commanding officer's home, later used by LSU's presidents. There were about twenty other buildings—officers' quarters, storehouses, magazines and the like—that were modified for university use.

Unfortunately, Boyd's troubles with the Board of Supervisors were worse than ever. Neither Governor Samuel McEnery, the ex-officio board president, nor

1888

LSU establishes first experimental station—for sugar planters in Kenner. Moves to Audubon Park in New Orleans the following year.

1890

Congress passes second Morrill Act. Louisiana has option of integrating LSU or establishing a separate land-grant college for blacks. Opts for latter, splitting new Morrill funds between LSU and Southern University.

Leon Jastremski, the vice-president, favored the relocation, because the board lacked the necessary funds to clean up the grounds and move in. Boyd agreed with the executive committee that all plans to move should be shelved until the General Assembly came up with the necessary funding.

But Boyd did not wait. He took it upon himself to have the neglected Arsenal buildings cleaned and painted, and to have university equipment and supplies hauled from the old campus to the new. He accomplished the move without notifying the board until their October 4, 1886, meeting, the day before the fall semester's scheduled opening. His failure to keep the supervisors informed left him in an untenable position. The board not only reprimanded him, but initially refused to reimburse him for the $1,800 expended. In November, the disheartened Boyd submitted his letter of resignation. The new interim president turned out to be Boyd's much younger brother, Thomas Duckett Boyd.

David Boyd changed his mind and tried to retract his resignation in April 1888. The board responded by offering Thomas Boyd the permanent presidency. Since David still coveted the position, Thomas withdrew his name from consideration. The board rehired former president James W. Nicholson. By mid-1888, the

On May 13, 1893, LSU played its first intercollegiate baseball game against Tulane. The Tigers won 10–8. Photograph by Andrew Lytle.

LSU played its first home football game (team pictured here) against Ole Miss on December 3, 1894. LSU lost 26–6, even with new coach A. P. Simmons playing in the backfield. Courtesy of Charles East.

Boyd brothers had departed—David to head a military school in Kentucky, and Thomas to become president of the new State Normal School in Natchitoches (now Northwestern State). David Boyd had resolved two major problems at LSU, making peace with the Grange and moving into a permanent home. Nicholson, who remained president until 1896, resolved a third—continuity of leadership.

Justin Smith Morrill, in 1890 at the age of eighty, pushed his Second Morrill Act through Congress. While the original Morrill Act initiated the land-grant college concept, the second one expanded its scope and ensured its permanence. It also bolstered the education of "colored students" by prohibiting racial discrimination.

Those land-grant schools not already integrated had a choice of either desegregating their existing facilities or opening a separate college for blacks. Louisiana,

fifteen other states, and one territory adopted this latter course—establishing the "separate but equal" doctrine in higher education six years before *Plessy v. Ferguson.*

Southern, the state's existing black university, became Louisiana's second land-grant school, soon to share the new Morrill funds with LSU. Meanwhile, the assembly established two industrial institutes for whites, one in Ruston (now Louisiana Tech) and another in Lafayette (now UL–Lafayette).

Nicholson resigned his presidential post in 1896 and returned to teaching. The Board of Supervisors sought a replacement who could raise the university above the financial morass then engulfing the state. They turned to Thomas D. Boyd, now a forty-two-year-old LSU graduate who had already served his alma mater as professor, commandant of cadets, and interim president.

Thomas D. Boyd

7   The Downtown Campus

Thomas Boyd honed his administrative skills while at the State Normal School—working closely with his faculty, strengthening his ties with the community, maintaining discipline on campus, and, above all, squeezing funds from the cash-strapped General Assembly. Now he brought his talents to LSU, where he found the top priority was attaining higher appropriations to meet increased demands.

Meanwhile Thomas Boyd suffered a great personal loss. David Boyd had not found steady employment since resigning from LSU, though he dreamed of being a college president again. Thomas Boyd hired his older brother as a faculty member. It must have been hard for David to serve in a subordinate position at an institution he had once headed. Whatever the reasons, David Boyd worked himself to the point of exhaustion and died in May 1899.

LSU's financial situation improved over the next ten years. In 1904 the assembly removed the cap on LSU's annual funding. Congress increased funding for

These gates marked the boundary between the old campus and the city. Photograph ca. 1920.

1897

The present *Reveille* begins publication.
    Audubon Sugar School incorporated into a degree program at LSU.

1900

First state appropriation for new LSU buildings since the 1850s.
    First issue of the *Gumbo* appears.

BATTLE OF THE COLLEGES

In 1906, during Thomas Boyd's tenth year as LSU's president, Tulane University began to make waves. Tulane's first president, William Preston Johnston, a former LSU president himself, had worked closely with Boyd. But after Johnston died in 1899, the New Orleans school's finances went into a tailspin.

In 1904 Tulane picked a new president, the tough-minded Edwin B. Craighead, who was known for being long on aggression and short on tact. His inaugural speech left few doubts about his goals. "Tulane is a public institution, entitled to state support," thundered the new president. He then provoked a war with LSU. This conflict quickly escalated into a bloody no-holds-barred struggle closely watched throughout Louisiana. The press covered it as the "Battle of the Colleges."

The forum should have been the courts, but Tulane opted for the 1906 General Assembly. Though Tulane made the first move with a seemingly innocuous request for a $25,000 appropriation, its bid ultimately boiled down to one simple point: Tulane's status as a bona-fide state institution.

Tulane's legal team argued, with some justification, that Tulane had always been a state institution, and thus was entitled morally, if not legally, to state funds. Indeed, the secretary of state's office listed Tulane as a state institution in its yearbook. The governor, the state superintendent of education, and the mayor of New Orleans were ex-officio members of the board. The mayor as well as members of the General Assembly could award scholarships. As the successor of the University of Louisiana, Tulane had attained certain benefits under the state constitution, leading many to believe it was, at the very least, a quasi-state school and hence entitled to state aid.

LSU's attorneys relied on Act 43 of 1884, the act establishing Tulane (and later ratified as a constitutional provision). In a trade-off for receiving the rights and immunities of the University of Louisiana—such as exemption from taxation (state, parochial, and municipal)—the Tulane board agreed to waive all legal claim upon the state for any appropriation in favor of the University of Louisiana.

LSU's alumni and their counterparts at Tulane joined the fray, urging their respective alumni to step up their propaganda efforts. The battle at this juncture had become purely political—and nasty. Personalities and rhetoric, not issues, would determine the final outcome. In this, Tulane got the first jump. Governor Newton C. Blanchard, with close ties to both universities, lined up on the Tulane side.

As the House vote approached, the LSU legal team needed a knockout punch. In a desperate move, one which could easily backfire, they contacted Edward Douglass White, associate (later chief) justice of the United States Supreme Court, for his opinion. Not only had he been an original member of the Tulane board, handpicked by Paul Tulane, but he had prepared many of the original legal documents. His reply turned out to be a bombshell: *Tulane should neither seek nor receive state aid.*

White's telegram, though not becoming a part of the official record, was still read on the House floor—in fact, just minutes before the final vote. Their bill went down to defeat.

experiment stations through the Adams Act of 1906. Next, it raised Louisiana's annual grant under the Second Morrill Act (still being split between LSU and Southern) from $25,000 to $50,000.

Curricular choices at LSU also expanded. In 1897 the highly successful Audubon Sugar School moved to Baton Rouge. LSU could then offer a five-year course—with classwork on the Baton Rouge campus and practical study at the sugar experiment station in New Orleans's Audubon Park. In 1906 the LSU Law School opened. Boyd also explored the possibility of opening medical schools, but this would not happen until after his presidency. In 1908 LSU divided the university into colleges—Engineering, Arts and Sciences, and Teachers (now Education). The university also established the School of Agriculture and the Graduate Department. The new century brought on higher enrollment (approaching 400 in 1900 and topping 600 by 1907), better funding, and more student activities. The rejuvenated *Reveille* rolled off the press on January 14, 1897, following a twenty-five-year hiatus. The first *Gumbo* was published in the spring of 1900.

LSU needed more buildings. The Baton Rouge campus, relying on a wide array of aged army structures,

had run out of suitable classroom space. The state had allotted no building funds since the school's original antebellum building back in Pineville. Now two board members, William Garig and John Hill, donated buildings, Garig Hall and Hill Memorial Library. In 1900 the General Assembly finally underwrote a building campaign for LSU.

The first appropriation, $25,000, went to erect Foster Hall, a mess hall and dormitory. Other buildings followed, including Heard Hall (Physics and Chemical Engineering), Irion Hall (Chemistry), Robertson Hall (Mechanical Workshop), a laundry, and LSU's first power plant. Then the alumni raised funds for the new administration building, Alumni Hall. The board then tapped its own resources. Two tracts remained at the A&M College Farm at Chalmette. One was donated by the state in 1902 (but not transferred until 1907) to the federal government for the Chalmette National Historical Park. LSU sold the remaining parcel to a railroad in 1905 for $16,934.50, using $10,000 for a new engineering laboratory and most of the balance to bail out the Society for Alumni, who ran short in their fundraising efforts for the new Alumni Hall. Peabody Hall, funded by the Peabody Educational Foundation, was

Senior cadets shave the head of a young freshman as his comrades look on, ca. 1900. This long-standing tradition, which became a rite of passage for young men entering LSU, ended in the mid-1960s.

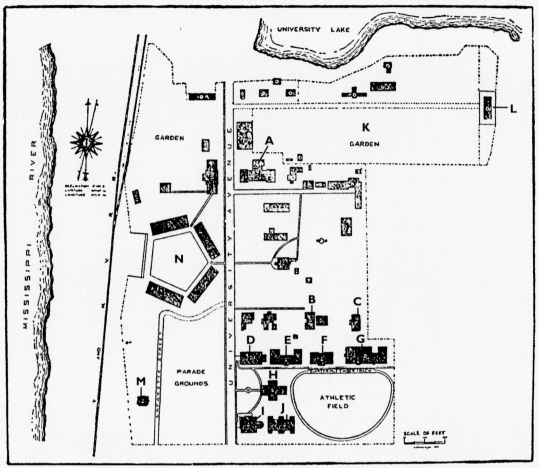

An LSU map, ca. 1902, updated by the author

The old Baton Rouge Arsenal had been home to LSU since 1886 with no new facilities being added until the turn of the century, when state and private funds financed a major construction program. Among the new buildings were:

A. Foster Hall
B.   Power House and Engineering Lab
C. Laundry
D. Garig Hall
E. Irion Hall

F. Heard Hall
G. Robertson Hall
H. Hill Memorial Library
I. Alumni Hall
J. George Peabody Hall

The first classes moved to the new campus in 1925; the last in 1932. Most buildings were demolished during the early 1930s, making room for the new capitol (K), but a few received a reprieve, staying around as state office buildings until after World War II. Alumni Hall was razed in 1934 and rebuilt on the new campus.

Zachary Taylor's long-time residence (M) had already been torn down, leaving only the Veterinary Hospital (L), formerly a Magazine and now the Arsenal Museum, and the Pentagon Barracks (N) as physical reminders of the Army Arsenal and the old LSU campus.

completed in 1915. LSU could then boast one of the South's larger physical plants.

Meanwhile, thanks to additional federal programs for land-grant institutions, LSU continued to make strides in agricultural training. The 1914 Smith-Lever act expanded on the "teaching by demonstration" philosophy of the renowned Seaman Knapp, whose rice-farming methods opened southwest Louisiana to settlers. Because of increased job opportunities as county agents and home demonstration agents, the act rekindled interest in agriculture studies and led to the initiation of home economics courses at LSU.

LSU continued to forge ahead, especially with its military program, taking pride in its Ole War Skule name. Under Thomas Boyd, himself a former commandant, the Corps of Cadets maintained discipline, though it was not as strict during the twentieth century as during the nineteenth. A big change came in 1916 with the passage of the National Defense Act and with it the birth of the Reserve Officers Training Corps. Once the university's participation became effective, a new level of professionalism was introduced. LSU joined the other schools in switching to army-issued olive drab uniforms, but it soon returned to the traditional West Point gray.

Boyd had another big change in mind for LSU: coeducation. While the idea of a coed LSU had surfaced in a Board of Supervisors meeting as early as 1881, it did not occur until 1906, and then in small numbers. But with Boyd as LSU's president, the outlook for women began to improve.

The Civilian Rifle Team takes aim.

Built with ten thousand dollars donated by wealthy commission merchant William Garig, Garig Hall was the center of social life on the old campus. Assemblies, chapel services, dances, pep rallies, and graduations took place inside the walls of this red-brick building. The above photograph, ca. 1910, shows a group of people, perhaps students and townspeople, leaving Garig Hall. Photograph from the Eleanor Lobdell Photograph Collection.

Aerial view of the old campus, early 1920s.

The State Normal was coeducational. Of the 362 students during Boyd's last year there, most were women. Based on his eight years of experience as president of the Normal, he felt women students could easily fit into the LSU program.

In 1892, while at the Normal, Boyd had recommended to the General Assembly that a state industrial school for women be initiated on his campus. Against his wishes, two industrial schools were established, one at Ruston, the other at Lafayette. Both opened for men and women students, not for women alone. In doing so, at least they chiseled away at LSU's resistance to coeducation.

Closer to home, women attending the Peabody Normal program held each summer on the LSU campus were housed in the LSU Pentagon Barracks—the same facility quartering male cadets—without incident. The *Reveille*, soon after it resumed publication in 1897,

championed the cause of fully accepting women students, stating, "There is no good reason for excluding them—only a prejudice and a clinging to the dead past." Boyd agreed but moved slowly.

The first significant chink in LSU's armor came in 1904 with R. Olivia Davis's application to enroll in an afternoon calculus class. A graduate of Newcomb College, she taught mathematics at Baton Rouge High School. Rather than seeing a trend, the faculty viewed her request as a reasonable exception and agreed to accept her.

Later Davis sought and received permission from Boyd to continue a graduate program leading to a master's degree. When submitting her name as a candidate for a degree, he explained to the board how she had been a satisfactory student and, perhaps more important, had not distracted the male cadets from their daily activities. Olivia Davis became LSU's first female

graduate in the spring of 1905, rekindling the topic of
complete coeducation.

It remained a tough decision for board members,
but Boyd made it easy for them. Unless they specifically turned him down, he planned to open LSU's
doors to all female applicants. The board took no action. In the fall of 1905, another woman registered.
Now there would be no turning back!

A year later, thirty-one women responded to LSU's
call for coeducation. Seventeen were incoming freshmen from the graduating class of Baton Rouge High
School. Among them was Thomas Boyd's daughter
Annie.

One of two promissory
notes signed by two deans
and seven business leaders
when purchasing the Gart-
ness Plantation in May 1918.
They held the property until
August, when the state came
up with the funds to buy it
(for the same amount).

1904

R. Olivia Davis becomes first female to attend LSU—as a graduate student; receives master's degree in 1905.

1906

LSU opens its doors to undergraduate females. Seventeen
enroll.

1907

State transfers balance of the
A&M College farm property to
the federal government for a national battlefield monument.

II THE GREATER UNIVERSITY

A statue of Spanish explorer Hernando DeSoto once overlooked the reflecting pool at the base of the Greek Theater. In 1960, university officials decided to fill in the pool, which had become a dump site for students and a breeding ground for mosquitoes, and to replace it with a formal garden. Photograph from the Jasper Ewing Collection.

8   The New Campus

LSU had one of the best physical plants in the South. But Thomas Boyd dreamed of an even more spacious campus. In 1918 he heard that the Gartness Plantation, just south of Baton Rouge, might be put on the market. This was the ideal spot for a new campus, but neither the university nor the state had enough money to buy it. Although Governor Ruffin G. Pleasant was solidly behind the project, he had to wait until the General Assembly opened its session in mid-April to appropriate the funds.

Boyd, fearing competition from other prospective buyers, decided not to wait. He asked Dean Thomas W. Atkinson, long active in real estate, to enter negotia-

tions with the owner. Once a price of $82,000 was established, Atkinson acquired an option to hold the property until May 31, 1918. But this still did not give legislators enough time to act.

On May 22, to solidify public support, LSU invited the lawmakers and other prominent leaders to a barbecue on the Indian mounds of the Gartness property. The guests were impressed. But there was still the problem of money, and Atkinson's option expired in nine days.

Atkinson knew what to do. On the day after the barbecue, he, Dean William R. Dodson, and seven Baton Rouge business leaders—Robert A. Hart, David M.

LSU president Thomas Boyd (second from left) presides over a picnic on the site of the new campus.

1912

Airplane crashes on LSU campus.

1916

National Defense Act creates the Reserve Officers Training Corps (ROTC) with LSU becoming one of the first schools to participate.

PROPOSED
LOUISIANA STATE UNIVERSITY
BATON ROUGE LOUISIANA
Olmsted Brothers, Landscape Architects
Brookline, Mass. — October 1921

Bird's-eye view of the new campus as proposed by Olmsted Brothers in 1921.

Reymond, J. Allen Dougherty, Sabin J. Gianelloni, Ollie B. Steele, J. H. Rubenstein, and Benjamin B. Taylor—assumed the risk, exercised the option, and jointly purchased the plantation. They borrowed the money, signing two notes—one for $50,000, the other for $32,000.

The appropriations bill was signed in June. By mid-August, LSU was ready to acquire the acreage from the Atkinson group for the same $82,000 price. Even then, the state, short of cash, could only come up with $32,000. This permitted the university to retire one note while assuming the other. LSU, though not yet ready to start building, had its new campus.

On May 17, 1920, the colorful John M. Parker was sworn in as governor. Elected on a broad platform,

LSU President Thomas Boyd (center) and other dignitaries break ground for the Dairy Barn on the new campus, 1922.

Parker presented a far-reaching agenda—improving major highways (replacing dirt and mud with gravel), pursuing conservation and reforestation, initiating "blue sky" legislation to protect investors, regulating oil and gas, and above all, building LSU into a greater agricultural college. Parker's persistent efforts on behalf of the university earned him the title "Father of the Modern LSU."

Parker pursued a source of funds that previous Louisiana lawmakers had not tapped. Parker proposed a severance tax on all unrefined natural resources that were taken out of Louisiana for processing. A large portion of this money would go to LSU.

Early in 1920, between his election and inauguration, Parker appointed a Greater Agricultural College Committee to tour five schools to study their agricultural programs. Boyd selected the colleges to be visited: Clemson College and the Universities of Minnesota, Illinois, Wisconsin, and Tennessee. The last four institutions, like LSU, served both as their state's primary public university and its land-grant college. The com-mittee found these schools' agricultural programs thriving within this environment. Their report, as Boyd anticipated, pleaded for a stronger agricultural school—but one remaining an integral part of LSU.

During the 1920 legislative session, Parker's 2 percent severance tax was passed. LSU's share was earmarked for further development and maintenance of the agricultural department. The university used $97,590 to buy 930 acres of land adjoining the new campus, including portions of the Arlington and Nestledown plantations, increasing its total acreage to 2,130.

During its 1920 session, the General Assembly, renamed the State Legislature in the process, called for a constitutional convention, which convened in March 1921. The delegates dedicated up to $5 million in new severance taxes for LSU, to be collected between July 1, 1922, and January 1, 1925—and this time for use by the entire university, not just the agricultural department. The amount raised turned out to be closer to $3.5 million, but it was enough to fund the initial construction.

A newly built Parker Coliseum stands in the shadows of LSU's south gates. Photograph from the *Gumbo,* 1938.

1918

Deans Atkinson and Dodson, along with seven business leaders, purchase the 1,200-acre Gartness Plantation as future site for LSU, holding the property until the state can find necessary funds.

1920

John M. Parker sworn in as governor. With LSU as top priority, becomes known as the "Father of the Modern LSU."
LSU purchases 930 adjacent acres, increasing total to 2,130.

Rushed to completion so it could be used in the 1926 dedication, the Greek Theater became the site of many student assemblies and graduations. Before World War II, it could accommodate the entire student population.

The 1921 constitution also established, effective January 1, 1925, a half-mil property tax to generate up to $1 million annually for the university's maintenance and support. This tax provided close to $700,000 the initial year—seventy times the constitutional maximum when Thomas Boyd first became president.

LSU retained its own board. The other state colleges—Tech, Southwestern, Southern, and the Normal—went from separate boards to a single one, the State Board of Education.

Basically two-year colleges prior to World War I, these schools now offered four-year degrees, gradually gnawing away at LSU's dominance.

In 1920 LSU moved ahead with its initial planning. Jacob K. Newman of New Orleans, a friend of Governor Parker and the son of LSU's nineteenth-century banker, had worked closely with Olmsted Brothers for several years and highly recommended them. Through Newman, the firm was engaged to prepare LSU's preliminary plans, and he became the university's liaison with Frederick Law Olmsted, Jr. Selection of the Olmsted firm was a wise move. The firm had, in addition to Audubon Park in New Orleans, already designed more than 250 public parks. It also helped plan and design sixty university campuses, including Stanford and Cornell.

The Olmsted proposed plan for LSU and accompanying planning documents, developed after repeated visits to the site and consultation with a faculty committee, were presented in December 1921. The plan depicted a well-landscaped campus of several quadrangles laid out in an informal, parklike setting on the long bluff a mile or so east of the Mississippi River. Board members accepted the Olmsted master planning documents and asked the governor to appoint a building committee to hire the necessary building architects, contractors, and supervisors.

Members of the LSU dance team perform at the dedication of the new campus. *Gumbo*, 1927.

On April 30, 1926, President Thomas Boyd (standing) presided over the dedication ceremony of LSU's new campus. Seated on the stage (left to right) are: president of Tulane, A. B. Dinwiddie; state superintendent of education, Thomas H. Harris; state senator from East Baton Rouge Parish Charles Holcombe; Reverend F. L. Gassler of St. Joseph's Catholic Church; Governor John M. Parker; and Board of Supervisors member Edward J. Gay.

Parker appointed Deans Thomas W. Atkinson of engineering and William R. Dodson of agriculture to the building committee, giving the university a well-defined A&M slant. On March 29, 1922, the building committee broke ground for the new campus. The first building, the 13,000-square-foot dairy barn, was finished later that year. Starting with this building was a shrewd move, placating the farmers and those lawmakers interested chiefly in agriculture.

On August 1 the building committee hired seventy-two-year-old architect Theodore C. Link to design the individual buildings. By then the building committee had altered the Olmsted suggested plan to unite its two principal quadrangles in a cruciform layout. Why the committee made the change remains a mystery, but reducing costs was one likely reason.

Though less famous than the Olmsted firm, Link was a prominent architect. His Union Station in St.

Louis, completed in 1894, brought worldwide acclaim. Other works of note included the Washington University Hospital in St. Louis and the Mississippi State Capitol in Jackson.

Link's plan utilized the same Olmsted site for the classroom core. The most striking design feature was two intersecting quadrangles which formed the cruciform enclosure. The larger quadrangle spanned a distance from north to south of one-fifth of a mile. The cloistered sides provided protection from rain and the summer sun. The plaza, site of the campanile, became the gateway to the quadrangles.

Such ancillary structures as the beef barn, a stock-judging pavilion, a freight warehouse, the laundry, and a power house were built in 1922 and 1923. The architect chose sand-mold brick in muted earth tones to blend with the main buildings. Soon came water lines, a sewerage system, and a mile-long tunnel for utilities.

1921

State approves new constitution, providing taxes sufficient to ensure LSU's construction and for future operations. Other state colleges placed under the State Board of Education.

1921

LSU selects campus plan prepared by Olmsted Brothers.

1922

LSU replaces the plan by Olmsted Brothers with one prepared by Theodore Link, who emphasizes Northern Italian Renaissance architecture in his formal quadrangles. LSU breaks ground for new campus.

1922

First homecoming celebration.

MAP OF THE NEW CAMPUS

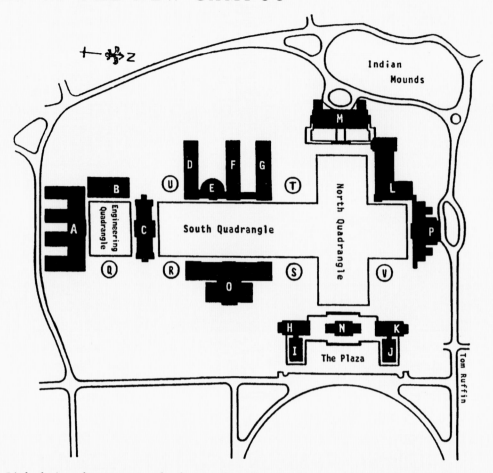

The Link-designed campus revolved around its classroom core—the Quadrangles. Remarkably, these buildings—shown with their earlier (and current) names and approximate dates of contract—were completed before the 1926 dedication:

A. Engineering Shops	December 1922	**The Administration Group:**		
B. Engineering Laboratory (Design Center)	January 1923	H. David F. Boyd Memorial	April 1923	
C. Main Engineering Building (Atkinson)	March 1923	I. South Administration (David F. Boyd)	April 1923	
		J. North Administration (Thomas D. Boyd)	April 1923	
The Agricultural Group:		K. Law Building (Thomas D. Boyd)	April 1923	
D. Biology (Audubon)	March 1923	L. George Peabody Hall	June 1923	
E. Agricultural (Dodson) Auditorium	March 1923	M. Hill Memorial Library	July 1923	
F. Agronomy and Animal Industry (Stubbs)	March 1923	N. The Campanile, or Memorial Tower	November 1923	
G. Home Economics (Prescott)	March 1923	O. Chemistry Laboratory (Coates)	January 1924	
		P. Murphy J. Foster Hall	November 1924	

Five more were added during the 1930s at the sites indicated—Geology (Q), Nicholson (R), Himes (S), Allen (T), and Agricultural Administration (U). Thomas D. Boyd Annex (V) did not appear until the late 1950s.

Although classroom buildings are now scattered around the campus, the Quadrangle remains a refuge, where students still walk freely without confronting vehicular traffic.

Link then turned to the academic halls, which were designed to accommodate a student enrollment of five thousand. Employing a sixteenth-century Northern Italian Renaissance style, Link designed his two-story buildings on the north and south quadrangles, referred to as the quadrangle or the court, with tile roof and a stucco finish. Adding his stucco finish increased the cost by $400,000 for the first thirteen buildings alone—a hefty percentage. But this exposed aggregate and the pebbly finish gave the central classroom nucleus the Mediterranean look for which LSU is known.

On November 1, 1923, shortly before his seventieth birthday, Boyd submitted his resignation. He still retained the respect of his faculty, students, and board, but was tired and ready to slow down. The timing seemed to be ideal. Theodore Link, whom he respected, was progressing on schedule, and just days earlier, had completed the final plans for his masterpiece, the campanile (N), or memorial tower. But eleven days later, on November 12, Link died. Major construction decisions still had to be made, and Boyd chose to postpone his retirement. The campanile was begun that month. Meanwhile, Link's son Clarence took over his father's role as supervising architect but was later replaced by Louisiana firms.

Construction on the football stadium began in 1924. The reinforced concrete stadium was located just below the bluffs so that its height would not overpower the two-story quadrangle buildings. Work on the chemistry laboratory (O) also began in 1924. Then LSU ran short of cash.

Parker's term ran out and Henry L. Fuqua became governor in 1924. Huey P. Long, in his first try for governor, ran third. Fuqua, a former merchant then serving as warden of the state penitentiary, was Boyd's brother-in-law. He was also an LSU alum, first enrolling at the amazing age of ten. Already sympathetic to LSU's needs, Fuqua kept the building program on track. In recognition of Parker's past leadership, the supervisors asked him to remain on the building committee.

The contracting company for the new stadium failed, leaving the bonding company to finish the job. With the structure nearing completion in November 1924, LSU capitulated to fan pressure. The university hosted the annual Thanksgiving Day clash with Tulane

in the unfinished stadium. More than 17,000 people, a Louisiana football attendance record at the time, watched the game. It was also broadcast on KFGC, LSU's new radio station.

The structure was tentatively called Tiger Stadium. The options narrowed to two, both honoring supportive governors. One was Parker Pavilion, the other, Fuqua Field. Although a heated debate followed, neither side prevailed. It's still Tiger Stadium.

Fans were impressed by the new quadrangles and the campanile chimes, which were heard that day for the first time. Although the Tigers lost the football game to Tulane, the new campus was a clear winner.

Groundskeeper/band director F. T. "Pop" Guilbeau (left) stands in front of the band hall in this March 1926 photograph. In 1930, Huey Long, who wanted to "jazz up" the band, demanded Guilbeau's removal as director. On March 19, 1958, a fire destroyed the wood-framed band hall.

Murphy J. Foster Hall (P) was placed under contract a few days after the game, but the new Pentagon Barracks did not go to bid until June 1925. Neither would be ready for the September opening. Nor would the Greek Theater, which saw an earlier bid opening aborted when white contractors boycotted a minority bidder. The amphitheatre went to bid again in December 1925, this time successfully.

Amazingly, LSU was able to complete and occupy the Memorial Tower and the first fifteen quadrangle buildings, including Foster Hall, before the close of the 1925–26 school year. Then quadrangle construction came to an abrupt halt because of declining severance-tax dollars. Too, an adverse court ruling forced LSU to give up $350,000 in disputed revenues. Although Link had projected six additional buildings, LSU could not

1923

1924

1925

Link completes plans for his masterpiece, the Memorial Tower, days before his death.

LSU plays first football game (vs. Tulane) in new Tiger Stadium. First live tiger mascot, Little-Eat-'Em-Up, steals the show.

Classes begin on new campus, although some remain on old campus in town. Women, residing on campus for first time, occupy vacated buildings on old campus.

Baton Rouge Electric Company provided scheduled bus service from the new campus to Stroube's Drug Store in downtown Baton Rouge.

fund the first five (Q, R, S, T, and U) until the 1930s, and the sixth (V) until the late 1950s. The consequence was that LSU faced an acute shortage of classrooms. Space had to be parceled out. The College of Arts and Sciences used Hill Memorial Library for foreign language classes. It also shared part of Peabody Hall, whose primary occupants were the Teachers College (now College of Education) and its Demonstration (now University) High School. The geology department occupied the home economics building and journalism the biology building. Yet they were better off than music and other schools, which temporarily remained on the old downtown campus.

Students were thrilled to begin the 1925–26 school year at the huge new campus. It was much different from the crowded downtown campus, and also much different from LSU today.

The campus was located in pastoral surroundings, two miles out in the country. Cattle grazed below the bluff. Most sidewalks were gravel. The "stately oaks" referred to in the current alma mater had yet to be planted, although many of the "broad magnolias" were here already. Only after school opened were telephones installed, forty temporary ones. Permanent phones had to wait. Some buildings lacked lighting fixtures. Air conditioning was years away. The library, the bookstore, and a number of other facilities had not been

completed. Nor had the cafeteria, billed as the world's largest. Yet it managed to offer limited service.

When the 1925–26 session started, all residential students continued to live on the old campus. The university moved the cadets to the new campus early in 1926 but had no immediate plans for the women. In fact, the women had just moved onto the old campus. The women occupied a dormitory converted from a vacated engineering building. Two other surplus buildings were soon pressed into service. At least housing was affordable, at one dollar per week.

LSU maintained its military discipline and its nickname, "the Ole War Skule." Thanks to the military, dormitory life was quite structured. All freshman and sophomore males, with few exceptions, were required to serve in the ROTC and, unless they were town students, live in the barracks. Rooms were to be cleaned and ready for inspection by 7:30 each morning. In the evenings, the barracks had quiet time for studying. Cadets leaving the campus in the evenings or on weekends had to be in full uniform. And under no circumstances were they to visit "places of objectionable resort."

The women, or "coeds" as they were generally called, were not under the military regimen but faced similar early-hour curfews. Freshman and sophomore coeds continued to attend classes on the old campus;

juniors and seniors, although living on the old campus, went to classes on the new one. Many jokingly referred to their facilities as the *Louisiana State Feminary,* a takeoff on an earlier school name.

The old campus was far from dull. Dancing had just returned to LSU after being banned in 1918. The lack of a gymnasium on the new campus relegated all dances to the old campus. The administrative offices remained in the old Alumni Hall. The Young Mens Christian Association (YMCA), center of the school's social and religious activities, likewise stayed downtown. The university library had a downtown branch.

A cadet could escort a date to a downtown movie, share an ice cream soda, and enjoy a pleasant walk back to campus, all for a dollar. Or they could take a moonlight ferry ride for a nickel each. Attending athletic events was tougher. Students living downtown had to travel to the new campus for football, but a respectable 5-3-1 season made it worthwhile. An added incentive was seeing the brand new mascot, a pre-Mike tiger named "Little-Eat-'Em-Up." Spectators had to go to Baton Rouge High School for basketball, where they sat in the auditorium to watch games being played on the stage. Baseball was played on the downtown campus.

At first, students commuting between campuses re-

lied on the 7:25 A.M. Yazoo and Mississippi Valley Railroad's shuttle train to reach classes. So did professors who lived on or near the downtown campus. Other professors began to build in the recently opened subdivisions, such as College Town, just south of the new campus.

With the hard surfacing of Highland Road from the city limits (South Boulevard) to the campus that October, Baton Rouge Electric Company's busses (the company's streetcars did not reach either campus) offered service every fifteen minutes. With daily revenue dipping below seventeen dollars, the rail shuttle was dropped. But there was also new competition for the busses—automobiles. Initially, the gravel River Road was the sole automotive access to the new LSU. Dalrymple and Nicholson Drives were years away. Automobile dealers reported record sales to students, however, selling more than two hundred used Model T Fords at an average cost of seventy-five dollars each. The more enterprising buyers defrayed their expenses by establishing jitney service between the two campuses.

Students took the obstacles in stride, completely oblivious to the problems still facing the administration. School officials delayed the official dedication until April 30, ostensibly to mark the anniversary of the

Murphy J. Foster Hall on the new campus served as the student union. Currently, it houses the Museum of Natural History, the Foster Hall Art Gallery, and a small café.

1926

1927

Cadets move from Pentagon Barracks on old campus to Pentagon barracks on new campus. New campus is formally dedicated.

The Boyd eras end as Tom Boyd steps down. Either he or his older brother David had served in turns as president forty-eight of the previous sixty-two years.

THE STUDENT, 1925–26

The student of 1925–26, when compared to today's, was younger and less sophisticated but better disciplined. The minimum admission age of sixteen was frequently waived, leaving many to graduate from LSU before reaching twenty-one, the voting age at that time.

Students were not as well educated upon reaching LSU. Most school systems offered only grades one through eleven, adding the twelfth grade much later. Many rural high school teachers lacked a college background, much less a degree. In the cities, a two-year normal degree usually sufficed. Until 1928 Louisiana's elementary and high school students had to buy their own textbooks, the quality of which varied from parish to parish.

Entrance requirements were simple: sixteen credits and a diploma from a state-approved high school. Higher math and advanced science courses were not around then, making compliance much easier.

Tuition was free to any U.S. citizen. Student fees, counting room but not board, ran less than $100 per school year. Meals in the university dining hall ran another $18 or so each month, depending on one's appetite. The old beneficiary cadet program remained in effect with parish police juries appropriating between $150 and $250 a year to worthy recipients.

Students generally selected their majors early. Entering freshmen joined the college of their choice without first matriculating in a junior division. Many had to undertake remedial work.

LSU had no medical school then, but did have an accredited law school. Law students had to be at least eighteen and either hold a bachelor's degree or have completed a two-year pre-legal curriculum. "Students intending to practice in Louisiana are strongly advised," according to the LSU Catalogue, "to acquire a sufficient knowledge of the French language to enable them to make use of the French authorities of the civil law."

Few enjoyed access to automobiles. Even those who had them generally opted for the trains and busses when traveling home from LSU. Most of the state's paved roads were located around metropolitan New Orleans and in Caddo Parish, with few others in between. Reaching New Orleans by car took several hours via the meandering River Road; a trip to Shreveport, crossing the Mississippi River by ferry at Port Allen and the Atchafalaya at Melville, was an all-day ordeal. Thus weekend trips home, which required special permission anyway, were infrequent. Keeping in touch with one's family usually meant a letter or a penny postal card.

One in four students was Methodist, ranking just ahead of the Roman Catholics. Baptist, Presbyterian, Episcopalian, and Jewish faiths followed in that order. About 80 percent were male.

Students enjoyed reading. Zane Grey was by far their favorite author, with Rex Beach second. They kept up with campus activity through the twice-weekly *Reveille;* the campus comic magazines, *The Purple Pel* and the *Giggler,* and the YMCA's popular guide, the *L Book.* For news of the outside world, they read the *State Times* or the new morning newspaper, the *Morning Advocate,* which began publication in August 1925, the month before classes began.

In 1920, LSU's College of Agriculture sponsored this agricultural exhibit car. Demonstration agents traveled around the state in this mobile classroom and introduced new techniques aimed at increasing production—crop rotation, fertilization, and seed selection—to Louisiana farmers.

Louisiana Purchase, Louisiana's statehood, and, in recognition of LSU's relationship with the federal government, George Washington's first inauguration (which by design, not coincidence, fell on the same anniversary date). The real reason was LSU's infrastructure was simply not yet in place.

The ROTC infantry regiment and the thirty-three-piece cadet band, major participants in the activities, could not move from the Pentagon Barracks on the old campus until the completion of the Pentagon Barracks on the new campus. The new ROTC uniforms, purchased by the students for $52.75 each, had also been delayed. Mrs. B. F. Toler, matron of the boarding department, was ready, but Foster Hall, where the cadets would eat, was not.

In spite of these delays, the dedication still came off

A group of coeds dance for spectators, possibly during halftime of a Tiger football game, ca. 1920. Photograph courtesy of the Louisiana State Library.

Aerial view of the campus, ca. 1930. The buildings of the Agricultural Group are pictured in the forefront (from right to left and identified by their current names) Prescott Hall, Stubbs Hall, Dodson Auditorium, and Audubon Hall. An unenclosed Tiger Stadium looms behind them.

"Just Stadium Rats." *Gumbo*, 1928.

on schedule. On Friday morning, April 30, 1926, in front of the memorial tower, the new campus and buildings were formally dedicated by university and state leaders. Following this came a separate dedication of the tower itself, conducted by American Legion officials.

After the Friday morning dedications ended, the overall program stretched out for two more days. Parades, concerts, dancing programs, banquets, and presentations followed. Then came the speeches from visiting dignitaries. And more speeches. The only hitch came when rain threatened to spoil a Saturday-evening barbecue. The guests simply moved from the Indian mounds to the quadrangle's cloistered passageways.

Boyd did not let the construction or dedication slow LSU's progress in other areas. The *Reveille* went from weekly to semiweekly, claiming to be the first college paper in the South to do so. Journalism was upgraded from a department to a school offering a four-year-degree program. The university accepted a donation of one thousand acres near Bogalusa for its forestry school. The student body successfully fought the Jordan Bill, which threatened to split LSU permanently into two colleges, one all-male and the other all-female.

The dedication of the new campus marked the high point of Thomas Boyd's career, but the move took its toll. As the 1925–26 school year drew to a close, he again submitted his resignation. This time the Board of Supervisors reluctantly accepted it, but he stayed on until Thomas W. Atkinson took over as president in 1927. Boyd had given more than a half-century to higher education, the last thirty-one years as LSU's president.

As president emeritus, he and his wife, Annie, continued to occupy their campus home on Third Street. Boyd walked each day to his old Alumni Hall office to work on his correspondence and papers. He also cleared up some of LSU's lingering problems. One involved title to the old campus, which the federal government had donated to LSU for educational purposes only. A complete move to the new campus could subject the old one to forfeiture. Boyd, working through Congressman Bolivar E. Kemp and Senator Joseph E. Ransdell, was able to get the earlier restrictions removed.

LSU, now with an unencumbered title, was able to sell part of the old campus to the State Department of Public Works as the site for the new state Capitol. Erection began in January 1931. Two months later, Annie Boyd, an invalid for many years, passed away. Sadly and ironically, in November of that year, Capitol construction necessitated demolishing the Boyds' home,

forcing the lonely former president to move. In November 1932, he suffered a fatal heart attack.

As a final tribute, a somber Corps of Cadets, without its band or color guard, quietly led the funeral procession from the St. James Episcopal Church to Magnolia Cemetery. Here, to the sound of taps, Thomas Boyd was laid to rest next to his beloved wife, Annie.

In the early 1930s, many of the old-campus buildings were destroyed to make way for Louisiana's new state capitol. Photographs courtesy Louisiana State Library.

1928

Huey P. Long elected governor. LSU receives Class A accreditation from Association of American Universities. Federal government gives LSU full title to the old downtown campus.

1930

Huey P. Long elected to the U. S. Senate while still governor but opts not to take office immediately. James Monroe Smith named LSU president.

9 Before Long

The transfer of power after Thomas Boyd's long stint as president was rocky and drawn out. The Board of Supervisors voted down Arthur T. Prescott, Boyd's choice for his successor. This came as a shock, since Prescott was unanimously backed by the faculty. The faculty was especially irritated that the board openly preferred the new president to be between forty and fifty years old, eliminating the sixty-something Prescott.

The board may have had an ulterior motive. Having long worked in the shadow of Thomas Boyd, the board saw an opportunity to expand its influence. The members respected Prescott because he had served as board secretary for many years. Still, he was Boyd's protégé.

At its November 1926 meeting, the board announced a major coup. The new president was to be Colonel Campbell B. Hodges, a career army officer in his mid-forties. A native of Elm Grove (in Bossier Parish), he had graduated with honors from West Point, later serving as commandant of cadets at LSU, where he earned his master's degree. Hodges had been well received by both the cadets and the faculty. In fact, the *Gumbo* dedicated its 1913 edition to him. Meanwhile, a disappointed but loyal Prescott agreed to remain as a dean.

Currently serving as commandant of cadets at the United States Military Academy, Hodges appeared to be an excellent choice, one who could return unity to LSU, a school so steeped in military tradition. There was one catch. With almost twenty-eight years of service, he needed two and a half more years to retire on three-fourths pay. His benefits could be preserved, however, if Secretary of War Dwight F. Davis granted his request for a three-year leave of absence.

The selection committee's excitement soon turned to embarrassment. Davis, by law, could not release Hodges to hold a "civil office." Louisiana attorney general Percy Saint ruled that the LSU presidency was a university position rather than a state position, but U.S. attorney general John G. Sargent ruled to the contrary. The state's congressional delegation entered the fray, but the army held fast. With Hodges staying in the service, the committee had launched and wasted its best shot.

At its June 13, 1927, meeting, the board went into executive session to try again. Once more they passed over Prescott, this time to select another dean—Thomas Wilson Atkinson, age fifty-nine—as "president pro tem to serve until the president-elect shall assume office," leaving Hodges somewhere in the wings awaiting his turn. Since Atkinson's new position was an interim one, he would continue his role as dean of the College of Engineering.

Like Prescott, Atkinson had long been associated with the university. He received his Bachelor of Science

In September 1932, Elena Carter Percy of West Feliciana Parish drove nine head of cattle to the office of LSU President James Monroe Smith. While the cattle grazed on campus, Miss Percy traded them for her university tuition. After the resultant publicity, other students subsequently used the barter system for payment of fees with such commodities as cotton and chickens. *Gumbo,* 1931.

1931
LSU opens new Medical School in New Orleans.

1932
Huey P. Long resigns as governor but runs state in absentia. He likewise remains as chairman of the LSU Building Committee.

and Civil Engineer degrees from LSU (the CE was a graduate degree once offered by the university). As dean of the College of Engineering, he had transformed the college into one of the South's top engineering schools.

A year of leadership limbo magnified some lingering problems. One, a creeping malaise found in some departments, could prevent Atkinson from attaining his number one goal—full accreditation of the university. Heavy emphasis would be placed on the quality of the professors, especially on increasing the number with advanced degrees. Atkinson, having developed an enviable faculty for the engineering college, moved to do the same for the university, even if it meant firing the weaker teachers. Also as part of the accreditation process, Atkinson directed a switch to letter grades and improved the library.

In November 1927, Atkinson tackled another personnel crisis, this time in athletics. As a longtime member of the athletic council, he understood its operations well. Atkinson had even been honored by the Southern Intercollegiate Athletic Association, which

predated the Southeastern Conference, by serving as its vice-president for many years. In 1914, he was named chairman of the organizational meeting for the new Southwest Conference, which LSU later declined to join. As the 1927 season started, Atkinson signed football coach Michael J. Donahue to a new six-year contract. By the time the dismal season ended, Donahue agreed to resign. Atkinson then selected Russell Cohen, who would give LSU four winning, though not spectacular, years.

Another crisis came with the dismissal of Francis T. "Tad" Gormley, a popular and successful track coach. As a temporary expedient, Atkinson asked a faculty member—Fred C. Frey, an associate professor of sociology—to fill in for a year while continuing his normal teaching duties. Although his track team became conference champions that spring, Frey readily relinquished his coaching duties to a top-rated newcomer, Bernie "the Old Possum" Moore.

On the political scene, the 1928 election brought in a governor who would change Louisiana forever. Huey P. Long won the race, automatically becoming ex-officio

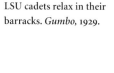

LSU cadets relax in their barracks. *Gumbo*, 1929.

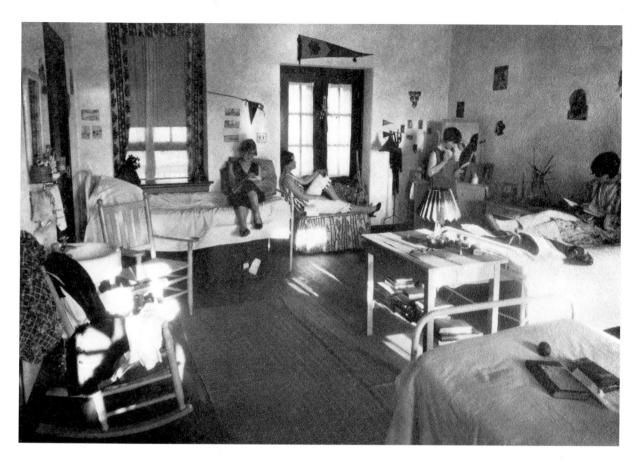

When the cadets moved into the Pentagon Barracks on the new campus, coeds moved into the Pentagon Barracks (shown above) on the old campus. *Gumbo,* 1929.

president of the Board of Supervisors. He attended his first meeting in June, primarily to listen. Few thought he would remain a passive governor for long.

In November 1928, Atkinson received the long-awaited announcement. The Association of American Universities had awarded its full Class A accreditation to LSU. The university was elevated overnight to a new level of recognition shared by such select area universities as Vanderbilt, Texas, and Tulane. For the first time, LSU's credits would be accepted nationwide. Accreditation was perhaps the high point of Atkinson's career; he had accomplished what neither the Boyd brothers nor any other president had done.

Huey Long, sworn in as governor a few months earlier, had little to do with the accreditation but clearly appreciated the increased prestige it brought. He and Atkinson maintained a mutual respect for each other, with the governor keeping his hands out of LSU's academic affairs. Both realized this would soon change.

LSU, in the meantime, continued on its roll. The engineering school became recognized as a registered institution by the University of the State of New York. Other schools—such as journalism, library science, and law—took steps to become recognized by their peer groups. A new College of Commerce (now Business) was established with Dr. J. B. Trant as its first dean. Within a short period, it too received certification.

A high priority for Atkinson was to revive the campus building program. Enrollment, except for a slight dip during the 1928–29 year, continued its upward trend. The demand was still there, but the money was not. Other state agencies were tapping the severance tax, once reserved for LSU campus construction. Two junior colleges came under state control in 1928—Louisiana Negro Normal and Industrial Institute (now Grambling) near Ruston and Southeastern Louisiana, just forty miles away in Hammond. They, too, vied with LSU for state funds.

Next came the housing crunch. A proposal had been made to add male dormitory rooms under the football stadium, but Atkinson came up with a quicker and cheaper solution. He simply added a third bed in every room in the barracks, immediately increasing the capacity by 50 percent.

Women's housing was far more complicated. Women, still housed on the old campus and needing more room, began to eye the century-old Pentagon

Completed in 1910 as a memorial to David French Boyd, the Alumni Hall on the old campus housed LSU's executive offices. It was torn down in 1934, with the salvageable material used to construct Alumni Hall on the new campus. The latter now houses the Manship School of Mass Communication. Photographs courtesy Louisiana State Library.

Barracks once used by army troops and LSU cadets. With living quarters on the second floor and bathrooms on the first, and connected only by open balconies and outside stairs, the old barracks would require $97,000 worth of modernization. But Atkinson could find no acceptable alternative on either campus.

Another high priority was a facility for large student gatherings. School dances were still held in Garig Hall on the old campus and basketball games at Baton Rouge High School. The open air Greek Theater could accommodate over 3,000 comfortably, but only in good weather. Atkinson, to stretch LSU's dollars, opted for a combination Gym-Armory, securing a quarter-million dollars from the legislature for its erection. The building was placed under contract by early 1928 and ready for use a year later. Located at the edge of the bluff, both the main floor (the gymnasium) and the lower floor (the armory) were on ground level—the former on ground level with the quadrangles above the bluffs, the latter on ground level with the drill field below the bluffs.

A versatile structure, the gym level (which had a stage at one end) could be converted to an auditorium by using four thousand folding chairs. Without the chairs, it could be used for school dances and basketball games. It also contained a balcony that could seat fifteen hundred more people. Additional classrooms were needed, but because of limited funds, few were built. A new highway engineering (later the geology) building—used jointly by the university and the State Highway Commission—completed the engineering quadrangle. Then came the Dalrymple Memorial Building to house the animal pathology department, and about the same time, the creamery. It appeared to some that Atkinson was favoring the "land-grant" schools—i.e., agricultural and engineering—over the others. Yet these new facilities made it possible to move classes from the main quadrangle, thereby freeing up prime space for use by liberal arts and other departments.

During the early days of 1929, a number of events took place that quickly clarified Atkinson's nebulous presidency. President-elect Hodges, while commandant of cadets at West Point, had filled in admirably for the superintendent during the latter's illness. Even doubters now realized he could run a major institution. The LSU board still wanted him. Former governor John M. Parker, who had known Herbert Hoover since their Food Administration days, approached the new president on Hodges's behalf. So persuasive was Parker that Hoover appointed Hodges as his military aide rather than releasing him to LSU.

It was just as well. As far as the Kingfish was concerned, Campbell B. Hodges would never become president, not because of his actions, but rather those of his brother, W. H. Hodges—who was guilty in Huey's eyes of an unpardonable sin, having served as upstate campaign manager for Riley J. Wilson, Long's chief opponent in the 1928 gubernatorial race.

At their June 1929 meeting, the board members, to head off possible Long intrusions, decided to resolve the presidential stalemate. Hodges "was terminated and set aside on account of said inability to report," and Atkinson was named president.

Atkinson, as full president, saw little problems multiplying into bigger ones. During the spring of 1930, a scandal sheet, the *Whangdoodle*, stunned the campus community with a shocking exposé—identifying a popular LSU dean as a drug trafficker, then detailing his lurid affair with Brown Sugar, a sixteen-year-old prostitute. And this was not the only such revelation. The stories, though involving several different students and faculty members, had one thing in common—they simply were not true. Atkinson launched a full investigation, determining the ringleader to be Kemble K. Kennedy, a senior law student who had served as LSU's student body president and was currently holding down the same post for the Law School.

The uncovering of his role could not have come at a

A grader prepares the road bed prior to paving Nicholson Drive, ca. 1936. Photo courtesy of Louisiana State Library.

worse time for Kennedy, who expected to graduate in just a few days. Atkinson suspended him, leaving him ineligible to receive a law degree. Since Kennedy had been active in his gubernatorial campaign, Long tried to intervene. But Atkinson stood fast, refusing to let him graduate. Kennedy incurred a jail sentence in

Women's Athletic Association pledges. *Gumbo*, 1931.

BEFORE LONG

65

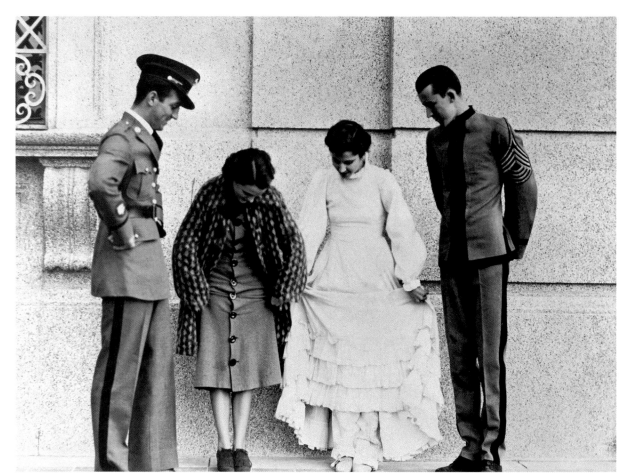

Comparing costumes: The cadet uniform and the white dress of the sponsor (couple on right) in pre-1918 style contrast with the contemporary style of the couple on the left, whose dress is typical of LSU students in the mid-1930s and 1940s, including the military rather than cadet uniform worn by the ROTC member.

November for criminal libel only to receive an immediate reprieve from the governor.

Atkinson's first three years had been difficult ones. His heart problems had been aggravated by the increased pressures of office. The specter of Hodges and the board's treatment of Prescott divided campus loyalties. A lack of support kept him off balance.

On the positive side, Major Troy W. Middleton arrived in 1930 to serve as commandant of cadets. Fred Frey was named dean for the first time. Both would later head the university.

Long appointed six new members to the Board of Supervisors in July 1930. That fall, he demanded that the band be increased in size from 30 to 125 members and that the grounds keeper/band director F. T. "Pops" Guilbeau be fired and replaced by A. W. Wickboldt.

The LSU administration initially demurred, but ultimately went along to a point. The band grew larger, Wickboldt became its new director, but Guilbeau was not fired. He remained on the staff in the grounds keeper role alone. Shortly thereafter, Atkinson suffered an attack of influenza, leaving him exhausted and unable to spar with the governor any longer. He tendered his resignation on November 7, 1930.

The board met ten days later, not on the campus, but at the executive mansion. It was the governor's show all the way. Atkinson, confined to bed, could not attend, but his resignation was accepted. Even then, the board slighted him. Instead of awarding Atkinson the same "president emeritus" title conferred on Boyd, it simply named him "retired president."

10   Kingfish U.

It was November 17, 1931. Huey P. Long had been governor for two and a half years, and had already escaped an impeachment, crammed his aggressive program through the legislature, become the most controversial politician ever to hit America, and been elected to the U.S. Senate earlier that month. So far, he had intruded little in LSU affairs, but this all changed that day.

Now controlling the LSU board, the Kingfish announced his handpicked president—James Monroe Smith, a forty-two-year-old dean at Southwestern Louisiana Institute. An LSU graduate with a doctorate from Columbia University, he received unanimous approval, becoming the first LSU president to hold a Ph.D. degree. The faculty called him "Doc."

Arthur T. Prescott, no longer under consideration for president, stepped down as secretary of the board.

Cadets bow down to the Kingfish. *Gumbo*, 1931.

1933

Franklin D. Roosevelt inaugurated. Once he views Long as an adversary, FDR cuts off all federal funding in Louisiana.

1934

East Baton Rouge Parish Police Jury drains swamp, creating University Lake. LSU acquires its first junior college, Northeast in Monroe.

Huey P. Long (in white) marches with "his" LSU cadets, c. 1930. Commandant Troy H. Middleton (pictured right) is also present. Photo courtesy of the Louisiana State Museum.

The regimental band drills on the Parade Ground. *Gumbo,* 1932.

Smith took over these duties as well, thereby, whether intentionally or not, putting himself in position to change the official minutes of future board meetings. Smith assumed his duties that day as the titular head of LSU. Behind him, but visible and vocal, stood Long, determined to leave his mark on the university. Smith charged ahead on the governor's program, always care-

ful to share the glory with Long. After all, the Kingfish now looked on LSU as his university, and no one—not the faculty, not the students, nor the public—should forget it.

The new president, well received by the campus community, also related well to his fellow educators. More important, he was accessible. In fact he became

the first LSU president to live on the new campus. Smith would listen, then come up with money to finance new projects or to entice star faculty members from other schools—such as Eric Voegelin, Cleanth Brooks, and Robert Penn Warren. Dispersing funds grew even easier for him once Robert L. Himes, LSU's tight-fisted business manager known as "Tighty," was transferred to serve as business manager of the state penitentiary.

The impetuous Kingfish occasionally meddled in academic affairs, but Smith could usually divert Long back to football and the band. Demanding the best, Long soon hired a new head coach, Lawrence M. "Biff" Jones, and a new band director, Castro Carazo, then relished the fanfare they brought with them.

The students could forgive the governor for his showboating. After all, he made it financially possible for them to leave the farm and come to LSU. And once

Coach Biff Jones gives his team an inspirational talk. *Gumbo,* 1931.

LSU celebrates its Diamond Jubilee. *Gumbo,* 1935.

here, they found campus life not only educational, but also exciting. Long arranged for low fares to out-of-town games, allowing eager students to travel by the train load. Thousands took advantage of a special six-dollar round-trip ticket to Nashville in 1934. Once they arrived at their destination, the Kingfish was there to lead the Tiger marching band. He even composed songs with Carazo, including school favorites "Darling of LSU" and "Touchdown for LSU."

On the academic side, LSU's new literary magazine, the *Southern Review,* debuted in 1935, about the same time as the *Journal of Southern History.* Each published authors of note and attained national acclaim. These publications quickly added to LSU's academic credibility, as did the new scholarly books from LSU Press, which was also founded in 1935. It was Smith, not Long, whose support made such publishing possible.

In 1934 LSU began to operate its first junior college. The Ouachita Parish Junior College, run by the parish school board since 1931, transferred its operations to LSU to become its Northeast Center (and later LSU's Northeast Junior College).

Sometimes the Kingfish overruled Smith and embarrassed the university. He pressured the LSU board to confer a law degree on the publisher of the libelous *Whangdoodle.* On principle, the Law School dean chose to step down.

Another Long fiasco happened in late 1934 when he tried to name Abe Mickal, a star football player from Mississippi, to the state senate. Some students saw the incident as a gag, but others viewed it as another example of Long's abuse of power. The *Reveille* printed a letter to the editor highly critical of the governor's action. Once Long read an advance copy, he ordered the state police to seize all copies of the *Reveille* from the printers and destroy them—an action upsetting the entire journalism school. With threats and even resignations, the squabble soon escalated out of control. By the time it settled down, President Smith had expelled twenty-six students. He later reinstated nineteen of them. The remaining seven finished their studies at the University of Missouri Journalism School, thanks to an anonymous donor later identified as J. Y. Fauntleroy, the 1905 *Reveille* editor.

The board established the LSU Medical School at New Orleans in 1931. Dr. Arthur A. Vidrine was selected as first dean of the new medical school. He held this position in addition to the superintendency of the New Orleans Charity Hospital. A year and a half after it opened, LSU's medical school received its "A" rating from the American Medical Association.

Buildings built during the Long years include Smith Hall (now Pleasant Hall), a women's dormitory; the Music and Dramatic Arts Building; the Huey P. Long Field House and Recreation Center; and the home economics cottage. To fund their construction, Long arranged for LSU to sell certain property and buildings on the old campus to the State Highway Commission for $1.8 million.

The Kingfish stepped down as governor and was inaugurated as a U.S. Senator in January 1932. Alvin O. King, president pro tem of the state Senate, served briefly as acting governor until Oscar K. Allen assumed office in May. Yet Long continued to run the state and, by extension, the university, where he remained chairman of the LSU Building Committee.

During mid-1932, he forged ahead with enlarging the west and east stadiums, adding 10,000 new seats to the existing 13,000, then adding male dormitory rooms underneath the latter. The stadium was finished just in time for the 1934 Tulane game. Enlarged to 23,000

In 1934, LSU students, with a "loan" from Huey Long, traveled to Nashville to watch LSU's football game with Vanderbilt. In this photograph, cadets hoist their mascot, a paper-mache tiger, onto the train.

seats, it still needed bleachers to accommodate the 30,000 fans who showed up.

Long sought federal loans from Hoover's relief program, the Reconstruction Finance Corporation, only to become embroiled in federal red tape. He later applied for aid under Roosevelt's relief programs, only to be rejected outright. Adding to the insult, the East Baton Rouge Parish Police Jury managed to tap federal funds to drain the swamp that created University Lake.

In December 1934, the stymied Kingfish moved forward on his own. Using the school's share of the corporate franchise tax and a million-dollar loan from the State Board of Liquidation, he announced his building program for 1935: O. K. Allen Hall to house the College of Arts and Sciences; the French House; an addition to the field house; Highland Hall for women, the first dormitory in the Evangeline group; and the West-Side Stadium Dormitory for men.

The year 1935, two years into his first presidential term, was a crucial one for Franklin D. Roosevelt, the

United States, and especially for Louisiana. Long's "Share Our Wealth" societies were out-promising FDR on give-away programs, elevating the Kingfish nationally as a possible candidate in the 1936 presidential election. Over the years, Long made no secret of his ambitions for the presidency; among other signs, his governor's mansion was a copy of the White House. Although unlikely to win in the 1936 election, Long could still be the spoiler, conceivably drawing away enough votes from FDR to elect a Republican.

Prodded in large part by Long's growing national popularity, FDR in mid-1935 postponed the Congressional summer recess to push through a wide array of far-reaching social legislation—the Wagner Act, the Social Security Act, the Banking Act, the Public Utility Holding Company Act, and the Wealth Tax Act.

Harold L. Ickes, the PWA administrator who was known as "the old curmudgeon," had already begun holding up approval on Louisiana projects for political reasons alone. An angry Long, to short-circuit Ickes's ability to block Louisiana projects, or at least out of spite, established the State Advisory Board with the power to kill all requests for federal loans and grants before they ever left Louisiana. Ickes responded by accusing Long of having "halitosis of the intellect."

The generally persuasive James Monroe Smith tried his luck with a personal visit to Ickes, but to no avail. As the acid-tongued Ickes recorded in his diary (July 16, 1935): "President Smith then asked why there had been so much delay in passing upon applications from the State College [sic]. I told him that some people believed that this wasn't so much an educational institution as it was a political institution. He announced that he took great exception to that statement and I told him that was his privilege." Ickes went on to record that Long "assured the country that Louisiana was alright economically and didn't need any help from the Federal government."

Less than two months later, the Kingfish was dead, cut down by an assassin (or his own bodyguards' bullets) in the state Capitol he built. The Kingfish's efforts during his last five years left him larger than life to his followers. He has been credited with building LSU into a major institution, which he did. Many people measure his success with physical structures alone, even crediting him with buildings he did not build. At the same time, his other accomplishments have often been ignored—enrollment, for example, doubled in spite of the Depression. But misguided recognition comes with being a folk hero.

In Louisiana, the university community worried about the future. The Long machine had many lieutenants, but no true second-in-command.

The study of engineering has been a part of LSU's curricula since its founding. These students are learning practical skills in the mechanical engineering laboratory, ca. 1935. Photo courtesy Louisiana State Library.

1935

Southern Review and *Journal of Southern History* make their appearance. The LSU Press is established. Huey P. Long assassinated.

1935

The City of New Orleans files for bankruptcy.

Views of the French House, which has an especially interesting history. Fearing that French culture and language would die out in Louisiana, the head of the Department of Romance Languages, James F. Broussard, championed the construction of a center for intensive study of the French language, literature, and culture. On April 15, 1935, French ambassador André de Laboulaye laid the cornerstone for the French House as part of the university's Diamond Jubilee celebration. During World War II, the French House served as the quarters for the officers enrolled in the Army Administrative School, which was located at LSU. After the war, the building once again housed female language students and foreign students. In 1968, the building closed, and vandals immediately began sacking it. A decade later, the state legislature appropriated money to restore the once majestic building, and on April 3, 1981, Ambassador François de Laboulaye, the son of André, rededicated the French House. For nearly two decades, it was home to LSU Press and Phi Kappa Phi. In 1999, the Press moved to W. Lakeshore Drive, and the French House became part of the Honors College.

11 The Smith and Leche Years

The Kingfish passed away during the wee hours of September 10, 1935. His last words supposedly expressed concern over his poor boys at LSU. If he did say this, he need not have worried. The university grew at a much faster rate during the four post-Long years than it had during the Kingfish's tenure.

Initially, confusion prevailed. O. K. Allen, governor at the time, died four months after Long died, which was shortly after Richard W. Leche's election as governor. To bridge the four months to Leche's inauguration, James A. Noe became the acting governor. Finally, in May 1936, Leche was sworn in for what was to be a four-year term.

Leche embarked on a building program which rivaled that of the Parker-Fuqua era and far surpassed Long's. His mission, it appeared, was to outdo the Kingfish at every turn. While Long had introduced free textbooks to elementary and high school students, Leche added free pencils and paper. When it came to buildings, Leche's accomplishments came through his new partner, one Long never successfully tapped—the federal government.

Roosevelt's people, still fearing the impact of the "Share Our Wealth" societies, wanted to make peace in a hurry. They approached the governor-elect and other key Longites with a proposal soon referred to as the "Second Louisiana Purchase." Washington agreed to call off the IRS investigation of key Louisiana politicians and to begin approving projects of the Public Works Administration (PWA) as well as those of the

Initially, the Law School bore the name of Governor Richard W. Leche. After Leche's conviction, the university removed the governor's name from the building. The Board of Supervisors subsequently adopted a rule that no university building could be named for a person who has not been deceased for at least two years.

new Works Progress Administration (WPA, which was later called the Works Projects Administration). Leche, in exchange, agreed to kill Long's "Share Our Wealth" societies, to aggressively support FDR in the November election, and to help rebuild the once-solid Democratic South. Leche eagerly complied, soon eliminating the State Advisory Board, allowing LSU and other political entities to file their applications for federal loans.

As for LSU, at the June 1, 1936, Board of Supervisors meeting, not quite three weeks after Leche's inauguration, President "Doc" Smith could already report, "The Works Progress Administration was now cooperating with the university."

The Democrats in Washington got what they wanted, victory in the 1936 presidential race. Louisiana received what it hoped for, an opening of the floodgates to allow the free flow of federal dollars into the state and LSU. The PWA put Charity Hospital back on track. New WPA projects pulled New Orleans out of bankruptcy. LSU witnessed heavy activity in campus construction. Yet few remember Leche's efforts. Circular metal plaques bearing his profile once adorned his buildings but were later ripped from the walls. Even Leche Hall, whose facade duplicated that of the Supreme Court Building in Washington, subsequently became simply the Law Building.

Interior view of LSU's Agricultural Center. Photo courtesy Louisiana State Library.

What made Leche's efforts possible were the two federal giveaway programs, the WPA and the PWA, with LSU becoming a major beneficiary of both. The PWA, headed by Harold L. Ickes, emphasized large capital-intensive projects. The PWA made outright grants to project sponsors (up to 45 percent of the cost

Built by the Leche administration with WPA workers, the Agricultural Center was later renamed John M. Parker Coliseum, after the former governor credited with being the "Father of the modern LSU." Photo courtesy Louisiana State Library.

Designed and planted by Baton Rouge native Steele Burden in the mid-1930s, this formal garden flanked the president's house. From the Jasper Ewing Collection.

The enclosure of Tiger Stadium's north end zone by WPA workers not only provided additional seating for fans but also athletic offices and dormitory rooms for over one thousand male students. Photo courtesy Louisiana State Library.

of approved projects, in LSU's case). The sponsor, after taking bids, awarded the contracts to outside contractors. Ickes, maintaining tight control, wanted the most for Uncle Sam's money. In fact, many accused him of moving projects too slowly.

In contrast, Harry Hopkins, a former social worker and now head of the WPA, felt that money should be spent, not saved. With the WPA, the sponsor, such as LSU, became the general contractor, hiring as many unemployed workers as possible. The WPA disdained the use of mechanical equipment or other labor-saving devices unless absolutely necessary. The state had to

1936

Richard W. Leche elected governor, reestablishing a working relationship with the Roosevelt administration. Federal funds begin flowing into Louisiana once again with LSU becoming the major beneficiary.

1936

LSU plays in its first bowl game, the Sugar Bowl. First of the "Mike" tiger mascots, arrives on campus.

Conrad A. Albrizio's art students paint frescoes in Allen Hall corridors.

match these grants, putting up over half the money. Leche always found the needed dollars, some of them from his new sales tax (referred to as a "luxury tax" to ease the pain).

One of the first of the WPA projects was the construction of the north stadium, which doubled Tiger Stadium's capacity to forty-eight thousand, with accompanying dormitories to accommodate another twelve- to fifteen-hundred male students. This project also put over three hundred jobless men to work.

Smith and Leche decided to give special recognition to the WPA through its national administrator, Harry Hopkins, and its state administrator, James H. Crutcher, in hopes of developing a closer relationship. The salute to the WPA came in a special pregame presentation just before the annual Tulane football classic that November. The LSU Band marched on the field

spelling out "WPA," then remained in that formation during the entire dedicatory program highlighting Hopkins and Crutcher. Fans packed the enlarged stadium. NBC broadcast the spectacle. LSU approved an honorary degree for Hopkins, climaxing an excellent public relations event for both the WPA and LSU.

After that, the WPA came through with project after project—including Nicholson Hall and the agricultural building in the quadrangle, the infirmary, Alex Box Baseball Stadium, and the Parker Coliseum. Federal money paid for improvement programs like drainage projects and paving streets and sidewalks on campus.

During the first three months of 1937, WPA workers, under the direction of LSU's building superintendent, George Caldwell, built the Physics and Mathematics Building. Now Nicholson Hall, it contains a rooftop observatory and is currently the home of the Department of Physics and Astronomy. Photos courtesy Louisiana State Library.

Class dismissed?
Gumbo, 1937

successive invitations to play in the Sugar Bowl. Leche enjoyed the fanfare. The band became his ally, never balking when it came to spelling "Governor Leche" on the field. As Smith did with Huey P. Long, the reserved LSU president was content to remain in the background, letting Leche enjoy the glory alone.

Another big hit was the new tiger mascot, Mike, who appeared on the scene in 1936. After a year of residence at the Baton Rouge Zoo, the tiger had a new home of his own across the street from Tiger Stadium. Also popular was the university's acquisition of its own country club. LSU purchased the front nine holes at Westdale Country Club late in 1936, the back nine a year and a half later.

Smith announced a major academic coup in May 1938. LSU Press was chosen by the George W. Littlefield Fund for Southern History at the University of Texas to publish the ambitious series *History of the South*. Even though the initial volumes did not appear for a decade, the selection increased the stature of the young press.

In 1937, LSU came close to adding its next junior college in Shreveport, but voters there rejected the idea. That honor went instead to the Lake Charles (later John McNeese) Junior College, which opened in 1938.

During the post-Long years, LSU's enrollment

PWA grants paid for Himes Hall, the Faculty Club, three of the dormitories in the Evangeline group, and the geology building, as well as new structures at the medical school and the junior colleges.

The athletic department also prospered. The first three years following Long's death saw a marked improvement in the football team, which received three

Degrees are conferred on new graduates in Greek Theater. *Gumbo*, 1937.

Huey P. Long Field House. From the Jasper Ewing Collection.

continued to increase, jumping to nearly seven thousand by 1937. At that size, it was one of the nation's largest universities. By 1937 it also had its own post office—University, Louisiana. LSU had become a more prestigious school, and more enticing to prospective students.

The National Youth Administration, through its Student Aid Program, provided part-time employment, paying fifteen dollars per month to students whose families were on relief. But most of the aid came from the state. Leche provided many jobs on campus as well as with state agencies at the Capitol. State automobiles even took the working students home so they could vote. With such assistance easing the financial burden on families, Louisiana slowly began to pull out of the Depression.

President Smith and his wife, Stella, enjoyed LSU's prosperity. Stella's reputation as a hostess spread

1937

LSU has its own post office: University, Louisiana.
Caddo Parish voters reject bid for LSU branch in Shreveport.

Louise Garig (1888–1935) belonged to the first class of coeds (1906) to be admitted to LSU. She graduated in 1910 and was the second woman hired to teach at the university—her sister Mercedes was the first. Garig taught English until her death in 1935. Garig Hall was built in 1938 as a women's residence hall.

Most dances, including this 1936 Military Ball, were held in the Gym-Armory.

board, and he still maintained an open-door policy on university matters.

LSU's economic prospects had never looked better—enrollment, salaries, and construction were all on the rise. Euphoria engulfed the campus. But Smith had taken up some devious and dangerous hobbies. He participated in a "double-dip" scheme where he and others sold furnishings to the university that it already owned. He became an avid collector of "hot" LSU bonds, over $2 million of them, from LSU issues which had been rescinded or canceled and should have been destroyed. He also counterfeited some bonds not only once, but twice—then forged signatures as needed. The bonds could be, and indeed were, used as collateral.

Late in 1936, Smith took his boldest step, one which led to his biggest blunder and, ultimately, to his downfall. In late 1937, he used his agent, James M. Brown, to open an account with Fenner and Beane in New Orleans in the name of "J. Monroe." He began to trade heavily in commodities, primarily in wheat futures—the buying and selling of wheat for delivery on a predetermined later date. Smith, as a novice in commodity

quickly. She entertained frequently in their elaborately furnished home and adjacent garden—and was herself entertained, here and abroad.

Smith's faculty members, noticing his rich tastes, still called him "Doc" to his face but "Jingle Money" Smith behind his back. Yet his position seemed safe. He worked well with the state administration and with his

1938

President James M. Smith starts to play the commodities market, using counterfeit university bonds as collateral.

trading, tried to match wits with other speculators, many of whom had traded full time for decades.

Heavily leveraged trading had many pitfalls. Even with the price moving up over the long run, a small pullback along the way could wipe out the customer's equity. But not when you have unlimited, though scurrilous, collateral. Smith was not a nickel-and-dime player; rather, through subterfuge, he acquired contracts covering over 3.5 million bushels of wheat, almost double the limit permitted by law.

By 1939, with war clouds gathering over Europe, Smith studied his charts, notes, and maps and decided, as did many others, that a major armed confrontation would soon break out, one which would ravage the European wheat fields. This would create a shortage of wheat, thus increasing demand. If all went as he expected, Smith could amass a quick fortune through his investments in wheat futures.

Instead, the wheat market tumbled downward. When his broker demanded additional equity in May 1939, Smith deposited more "hot" bonds, this time $375,000 from an issue originally approved for the Bienville Hotel purchase but canceled and supposedly destroyed before being sold. These bonds, to be in

"good delivery" (i.e., negotiable) form, required a legal opinion from a recognized attorney attesting to the bonds' validity as well as to their tax-exempt status. But Smith failed to come up with an acceptable document.

Founded in 1909, the Dairy Department initially owned four registered Jersey cows. As the size of the department grew, so did the number of cows. By the late 1930s, students studying dairy science ran a creamery on campus and sold a variety of products including milk and ice cream. In this 1938 picture, students bottle milk for sale or for use on campus. Photo courtesy Louisiana State Library.

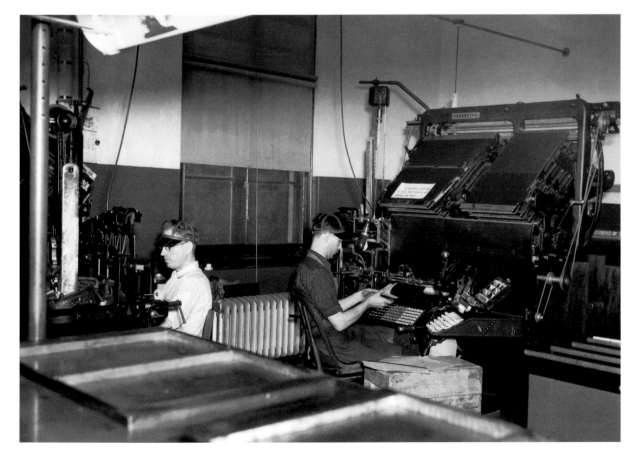

Staff members of the *Reveille,* LSU's student newspaper, set type in this 1938 photograph. The *Reveille* has been in print since 1897. Photo courtesy Louisiana State Library.

New Orleans. He borrowed another $100,000 from the City National Bank of Baton Rouge, and $100,000 from the Hibernia National Bank of New Orleans. Although the money was borrowed on behalf of LSU, the university never saw any of it. With his agent's help, the entire amount found its way to the brokerage house to satisfy Smith's losses of $458,039.97.

On Sunday afternoon, June 25, 1939, Smith called to make an appointment with Leche at the Governor's mansion, arriving there about 6:30 or 7:00 that evening. Smith told him about a $200,000 loss and asked for an opportunity to work himself out of his jam. Two LSU board members—state Supreme Court Justice John Fournet and Attorney General David Elliston—happened to be at the mansion on other business. Both nixed Smith's idea. Instead, Smith submitted this one-sentence letter: "I hereby tender my resignation as President of Louisiana State University and Agricultural College effective immediately," and departed for his home on campus. About 8:30 P.M., the

In this photograph, crowds of fans prepare to enter Tiger Stadium to watch their favorite team play. A brass plaque bearing the likeness of Governor Richard Leche hangs on the wall between gates six and seven. After the 1939 scandals, Leche's image was removed from the stadium and from other buildings on campus. Photo courtesy Louisiana State Library.

Fenner and Beane demanded fresh collateral, securities in good delivery, or cash to meet the almost $500,000 now due. Smith had already borrowed $300,000 from the National Bank of Commerce in

This 1938 photograph, looking west from the LSU football stadium, shows the LSU baseball field. WPA construction on the stadium and roads made LSU athletics events more accessible to Tiger fans. Photo courtesy Louisiana State Library.

state police issued an order for his arrest. By that time, Smith and his wife had vanished. At a 10:30 press conference that night at the mansion, Leche briefly told of Smith's resignation, his disappearance, and his apparent embezzlement of university funds. The story made the headlines in Monday morning's newspapers not only in Louisiana, but throughout the nation. The saga, as it unfolded over the ensuing weeks, turned out to be far worse—and involved far more people—than initially imagined.

Meanwhile, the Smiths were headed for Canada. Smith must have found this nationwide bulletin to be somewhat less than flattering:

DR. JAMES MONROE SMITH, WHITE MALE, 50 YEARS (APPEARS 60), 5 FT. 10 IN. . . . WANTED FOR EMBEZZLEMENT BY SHERIFF N. H. DEBRETTON, BATON ROUGE, LA.

The Smiths reached Canada, but soon voluntarily contacted authorities in Brockville, Ontario. Once the Smiths turned themselves in to the chief constable in Brockville, the Royal Canadian Mounted Police assumed control of the investigation and questioning. Smith and his wife were returned to the United States to face charges. Many faculty members still trusted Smith enough to stand by him. While he was being detained in the East Baton Rouge Parish courthouse, eleven people, nine from LSU, signed the bail bond for his wife.

Stella Smith went free, but "Doc" Smith was convicted and went to prison, as was true for several of his aides.

Former LSU president James Monroe Smith does his time at Angola following an earlier stint in a federal penitentiary.

LSU's airplane, ca. 1939.

12   Cleaning Up the University

As soon as the board members read their morning newspaper about Smith's embezzlement and disappearance, they headed to Baton Rouge for a special meeting of the Board of Supervisors. There they learned how Smith had pledged phony LSU bonds to finance his futures operations and then borrowed hundreds of thousands of dollars in the name of the university to cover his losses. After a long discussion, Leche presented Smith's resignation, which the board immediately accepted.

Leche introduced Dr. E. S. Richardson as his choice to replace Smith. A noted educator, Richardson had served as president of Louisiana Polytechnic Institute in Ruston since 1936, and before that as superintendent of schools in Webster Parish.

Richardson balked "at accepting a temporary" new

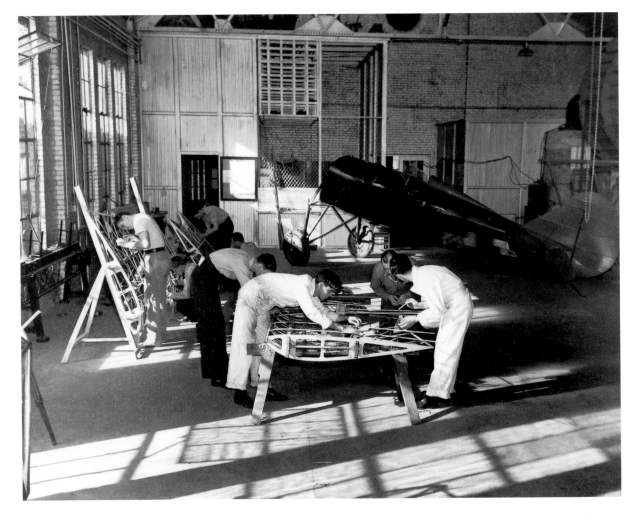

LSU students enrolled in the aeronautics program work on airplanes as part of their training, ca. 1940. Photograph courtesy Louisiana State Library.

Aerial view of the campus covered by a blanket of snow, ca. 1940. Photo by Fonville Winans.

office, one which necessitated his giving up the presidency at Tech. After assurances from various members of the board, Richardson accepted the appointment as Acting President, with the understanding that the board did not necessarily intend the position to be temporary. He accepted but immediately had second thoughts. The next morning, he contacted the governor to resign the LSU presidency, a position he held for less than twenty-four hours. Once back in Ruston,

Richardson told an overflow crowd, "I am here to stay. I'm not going to LSU. I don't care what they do."

When Richardson submitted his resignation to the governor, it was not to Richard W. Leche. During the intervening hours, Leche had resigned—the first Louisiana governor ever to do so. The new governor was Earl K. Long, Huey's younger brother.

At a meeting on June 29, the board accepted Richardson's resignation and approved Governor

Long's second choice for the acting presidency, Paul M. "Mac" Hebert, dean of the Law School. Dean of Administration Troy Middleton became acting vice-president.

But Louisiana would not be left to sort out this mess on its own. Federal investigators reached Louisiana even before Smith resigned and skipped the country. Their arrival was spurred by the June 9, 1939, edition of the *New Orleans States,* which published photographs of an LSU truck delivering university-produced mill-work to a private residence. This news would ordinarily have been ignored in a state known for such shenanigans. But the federal government couldn't ignore it once it attracted nationwide attention through the syndicated column "Washington Merry-Go-Round." New charges of the use of stolen WPA material on other residences, including Leche's, brought WPA investigators to the Bayou State en masse.

A few district attorneys aggressively pursued criminal charges. Trying to implicate Leche brought this terse response, "I deny any allegations and I defy my alligators." Other attorneys blocked every effort they could to root out dishonest politicians. Many state prosecutors ran scared lest the spillover drown them as well. Not too surprisingly, most of the early indictments were federal ones.

One of the first trials involved LSU's purchase of the Bienville Hotel in New Orleans late in 1936. Although the price included all the furniture, Smith conspired to have LSU buy the same furniture a second time for $75,000 (with $14,000 going to the Smiths). This amount paled in comparison to Smith's half-a-million dollars in illegal loans, but it was a start. In order to prosecute, the U.S. attorneys needed a federal angle and found it. Although the individuals charged had gone to great extremes to avoid use of the U.S. mails, they forgot that banks used the mails to clear their checks. The prosecutors remembered. In the end, Smith and the others involved were convicted of mail fraud.

It seemed that graft reigned at LSU—rigged bids, padded payrolls, mishandled budgets, embezzled funds, stolen building material, and kickbacks. Faculty morale sank to a new low.

The Paul Hebert–Troy Middleton team made the difference. Having them at the helm, LSU became one of the few state institutions to successfully clean up its own act. Corruption remained pervasive elsewhere in Earl Long's Louisiana, but not at LSU.

The Board of Supervisors had become a rubber-stamp board under Huey Long and Leche. Many members were office holders or state employees. After the scandals broke, the board took a determined approach to university problems. Only two board members resigned—Theo S. Landry, who also served as general manager of the state penitentiary; and L. B. Abernathy, the chairman of the state highway commission (Abernathy subsequently was charged with defrauding the university).

The board hired Franke, Hannon and Whitney, a New York CPA firm specializing in institutions of higher education, to audit the school's books. The firm

Panoramic view of spectators inside Tiger Stadium, 1939. Note that African American spectators are seated in the segregated section on the left. Photo courtesy Louisiana State Library.

Interior of a North Stadium room, ca. 1940. Photo courtesy Louisiana State Library.

found few records still intact, and those were antiquated, poorly kept, and rarely in balance. Physical inventories did not exist. Accounts receivables were in shambles.

In addition to straightening out the existing mess, the CPA firm worked closely with Middleton to centralize the handling of cash, establish a properly functioning office staffed by qualified personnel, and develop a bookkeeping system with the necessary checks and balances.

LSU hired three prominent Louisiana lawyers to work with the local district attorney to pursue civil litigation against those defrauding the university. By mid-October 1939, less than four months after Hebert took

Dressed in frock tailcoat and top hat, Porter "Eddie" Bryant walked the streets of Baton Rouge selling vegetables from a pushcart decorated with purple and gold streamers. He claimed that his vegetables, which were grown near LSU, were "educated" because of their proximity to the university and was given the moniker "Educated Vegetable Man." In the 1920s, Bryant became an avid Tiger fan when, according to him, the football team won a couple of games. When Mike the Tiger arrived in 1936, Bryant appointed himself the mascot's "manager" and often traveled to away games with the big cat.

Mike the Tiger with his trainer, ca. 1936.

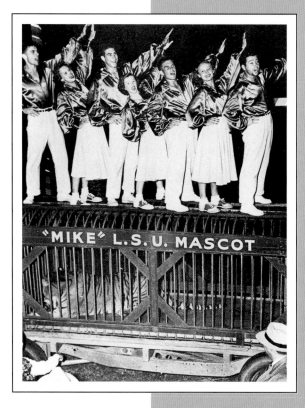

Mike's home has attracted thousands of visitors each year since 1936. Elevation plan courtesy of Somdal Associates.

WEST · ELEVATION

The seasons may change, the clothes may change, and even the Tiger may change, but the enthusiasm of LSU cheerleaders remains the same. These cheerleaders and Mike pump up the fans and the team in this 1950 photograph.

LSU used the nickname "Tigers" for nearly half a century before a live tiger mascot was brought to the campus. In 1935 the student body collected money to purchase the original Mike, who was housed in the Baton Rouge Zoo until a permanent home for him could be constructed near the stadium. Mike died of pneumonia in 1957, and students once again raised money to purchase another tiger. Mike II reigned for only one season before also succumbing to pneumonia. The third Mike lived eighteen years. His replacement, Mike IV, served the university for fourteen years before being retired to the Baton Rouge Zoo. Mike V, the current mascot, officially began his reign on April 30, 1990.

The cheerleaders and Mike II attract a crowd of students and fans to this piece of grass, where Lockett Hall now stands, behind the Agricultural Group in this 1950s-era photograph.

These Lambda Chi Alpha fraternity brothers take part in a parade on Third Street, which was the center of Baton Rouge's commercial district, to welcome Mike II.

Coeds collect money to purchase Mike II.

This 1937 picture of the LSU track shows the home of Mike the Tiger.

Mike V takes a break.

89

Until the 1960s, women were usually encouraged to enter the fields of education, home economics, or liberal arts. Basic sciences, business, engineering and agriculture were considered male pursuits. In her book *From Under the Magnolia Tree: A Family History,* Estelle Williams recalls this 1933 conversation with Dean Charles Pipkin:

> I explained that I had just graduated in June from the College of Education but that most of my undergraduate work had been in the College of Commerce and that I would like to get an advanced degree in Business Administration. Well, you would have thought a bomb had gone off in the office when he shouted: "Business Administration! Whoever heard of an advanced degree in Business Administration [for women]?" Glancing over my transcript he announced, "You'll get a degree in English." He then proceeded to fill out the necessary papers, and make a list of courses. I never said a word, but I was heartsick. I didn't want a degree in English. I didn't particularly like English courses. I had no real aptitude for English—and what could I do with a degree in English? Teach.

During World War II, women enrolled at LSU outnumbered men 1,815 to 1,710, and more of them enrolled in previously all-male courses. Olen Nance, a faculty member in the College of Chemistry and Physics, took this photograph of women working in a Coates Hall chemistry laboratory, ca. 1943.

Organized as part of the Women's Athletic Association, members of the women's rifle team were trained by ROTC officers and participated in national competitions. The Women's Athletic Association, which was founded in the 1910s, sponsored a variety of team and individual sports, including archery, volleyball, and hiking. The association encouraged participation by coeds in athletic activities. A women's rifle team from the late 1920s is pictured at right. Note: Women were not allowed to enroll in ROTC classes until 1967.

1939

Lake Charles (renamed John Mc-Neese in 1940) Junior College becomes an LSU branch.

1939

Louisiana scandals break. Smith resigns as LSU president, Leche as governor. Both ultimately sentenced to prison.

Interior view of a room in the Panhellenic Building. Each of the fourteen sororities on campus was assigned a room in this building, completed in 1938. The sororities held meetings, rushed new pledges, and had small parties in their rooms. *Gumbo,* 1940.

office, the legal team had already filed a number of civil suits and was in the process of filing several others. The amounts ranged in size from a few thousand dollars to three hundred thousand. Hebert then suggested the cases and potential cases be settled out of court wherever possible. The lawyers moved ahead accordingly, attaining excellent results.

The board members generally supported the Hebert-Middleton steps to clean up the university. Having placed their faith in the wrong man, they felt it was their responsibility to straighten out the resulting mess. In spite of LSU's almost unbelievable recovery, the Southern Association of Colleges and Secondary Education became involved. Its Special Committee of the Commission on Institutions of Higher Education dealt LSU a crucial blow in May 1940. It recommended that LSU be placed on probation until it reorganized on "a sound educational basis rather than on political considerations." The report also expressed a strong concern over the board's failure to name a permanent administration in lieu of the acting one.

Within days after the report was released, Louisiana had a new reform governor. The 1940 election was one

of the closest on record. Sam H. Jones narrowly defeated Earl K. Long. Jones led the broadest reform program the state had ever seen. He gave Louisianians three-dollar license plates, permanent voter registration, civil service, competitive bidding, an improved welfare system, and a corruption-free administration.

Yet his reform efforts at LSU turned out to be a double-edged sword. During his inauguration speech, Jones said, "The administration promised to fumigate the schools and fumigated they shall be, lest the very dream of political morality perish from this state." The governor proceeded to demand resignations from all members of all state school boards, including LSU's. Jones replaced the Long and Leche cronies with his own, and set out to eliminate signs of Longism on campus. The new board withdrew six honorary degrees, including the one for Harry Hopkins, approved by an earlier board. It issued a formal apology to the seven members of the *Reveille* staff dismissed from LSU by Smith and Huey Long in 1934. It fired bandleader Castro Carazo and discouraged the use of songs he composed with the Kingfish. The colorful band uniforms gave way to cadet grey, but women joined the

Students attending this Gym-Armory soiree dance to the music of the Larry Clinton Orchestra. *Gumbo,* 1940.

band for the first time ever. The board also discontinued the *Southern Review* and the *Journal of Southern History* and eliminated the Faculty Senate.

When it came time to select a permanent president, acting president Paul Hebert was the logical choice. Despite Hebert's qualifications, the governor had no desire to keep an Earl Long appointee, and Jones had already started to replace the other college presidents with his supporters. Those replaced included Dr. E. S. Richardson, who declined the LSU position in 1939 so he could remain at Louisiana Tech forever. To his chagrin, he found that "forever" lasted only two years.

For LSU's president, Jones selected the now-retired major general Campbell B. Hodges, who had first been

offered the presidency in 1926. He assumed office on July 1, 1941. Although once head of the U.S. Military Academy, he quickly discovered that running a major state university was also a special challenge. The general wisely designated the experienced Fred C. Frey as the dean of the university.

The Hodges and Frey team worked effectively together, especially after overcoming Governor Jones's attempts to manage the university. More political pressure, including some firings, came from Jones than from Leche and the two Longs combined.

Then came a larger problem, one for which they could not fully prepare. Five months after Hodges took office, the United States entered World War II.

1941

Japanese attack Pearl Harbor. The United States enters World War II. Male students leave school in droves to enlist. Female students at LSU soon outnumber men for the first time.

13 World War II and the GI Bill

LSU closed out a mediocre football season eight days before the attack on Pearl Harbor with a 19-0 upset victory over archrival Tulane. The existing air of exuberance rose to fever pitch once word of the Japanese attack reached the campus. Students thronged to the Greek Theater for an impromptu pep rally, where cheerleaders led them in cries like "Tigers take Tokyo." No one realized how poorly prepared the U.S. troops were. Most felt the Americans would be able to wrap up the fighting quickly. Caught up in the patriotic fervor, many students talked of immediate enlistment. If there was to be a war, no one wanted to miss it.

The student body marched as a group to the president's home. Hodges calmly explained that the war would be a long one and that everyone there would have a chance to fight before it was over. They could best help their country by remaining at LSU until they were needed. But keeping them in school would not be easy.

Over the course of the war, the Reserve Officers Training Corps (ROTC)—led by LSU, Texas A&M, and Virginia Military Institute—turned out officers in large numbers. LSU alone produced fifteen generals. The draft boards began pulling young men out of school

Cadets march in their weekly parade, ca. 1940. Photo courtesy Louisiana State Library.

Unidentified astronomers at the Clinton Observatory.

Enrollment dropped at an alarming rate, from a peak of 6,858 in 1938, to 3,105 in 1943. Even the professors, at least those not already in the service themselves, began to find themselves out of work. Some campus buildings gathered dust.

LSU and many other universities adopted an accelerated program in 1942. By lengthening their summer sessions to provide a year-round curriculum, schools could squeeze a four-year-degree program into three years. This worked especially well in Louisiana, where students at the time graduated from high school after the eleventh grade. It was possible for many students to finish their education at LSU before reaching the minimum draft age, which was still twenty-one at the time.

But in August 1942, the War Manpower Commission stunned the academic community when it issued a statement that "all able bodied male students are destined for the armed forces." Any further training would be up to the military.

Late in 1942, FDR prepared to lower the draft age to eighteen. At that point, his direct involvement in wartime education became a political necessity. In October, FDR asked the secretaries of war and the navy, not the educators, to explore how they might better utilize colleges and universities in light of rapidly falling enrollment. In November, FDR went a step further. He established a Post-War Education Committee to study and make recommendations on education after the war.

In December 1942, the army and navy jointly announced their plans for training programs that would find their way to over six hundred college campuses. The main two programs were the Army Specialized Training Program (ASTP) and the Navy V-12 Program.

The navy was already employing college campuses for its midshipman schools. With 131 participating colleges, most V-12 trainees could continue their education at their own or a nearby campus and continue the same course of study. New recruits came into the program as apprentice seamen. Those arriving from the fleet retained their rating and pay. Although in uniform, the V-12 trainees mixed with civilian students, took the same classes, and participated in the same extracurricular activities, including intercollegiate sports. A minimum work load of seventeen credit hours was required. To accommodate the navy, the schools

each day to serve as privates in the army or apprentice seamen in the navy. Those pursuing certain specialized degrees such as engineering were exempt. Still, many students hedged their future by dropping out of school early to enter either flight school or other officers training programs.

Others joined the Enlisted Reserve Corps (ERC), a program which recruiters claimed would permit students to remain in school until they graduated. Then, if qualified, they would proceed to Officers Candidate School (OCS). The Army's ERC attracted 606 LSU students, more than 10 percent of the total enrollment. Unfortunately, most failed to read the fine print, which stated they could be summoned into active duty earlier if needed. And needed they were. By year-end, these reservists were being called up.

1943

Another tradition ends. The cadet uniform in West Point gray for over eighty years, gives way to olive drab.

1944

Roosevelt signs GI Bill, which educates millions of veterans, thousands at LSU.
 Professor Robert Penn Warren wins Pulitzer Prize for his novel, *All the King's Men*.

"Howdy!" Cowgirls pose in front of the Agricultural Center in this 1940s-era photograph by Fonville Winans.

adopted a trimester schedule, consisting of three sixteen-week terms, two of those conforming closely with the normal sixteen-week fall and spring semesters. In general, college administrators found it quite easy to adjust to the navy's program.

The army's student training program was significantly different, down to its own special curriculum. All enlistees had first to undergo basic training. Those noncommissioned officers moving into the program were reduced in rank and pay to private. Once on campus, they encountered heavy doses of drilling, often marching as a group to their own classrooms. They found themselves isolated from the civilian students.

Worse, the ASTP students were not allowed to participate in intercollegiate sports. This placed the ASTP schools in a helpless bind, especially as they began losing their own athletes to the draft. In no way could they compete with the V-12 schools.

Football scheduling was so hectic in 1943 that Alabama had to cancel its entire season. LSU had to play

Georgia twice to round out its oft-changed eight-game season. During normal times, LSU's 5-3 season would not qualify it for Orange Bowl consideration, but it was one of the best "civilian" teams around. LSU not only was invited to the Orange Bowl but defeated Texas A&M after having lost to them during the regular season.

Tulane, Southwestern, and Louisiana Tech aligned with the navy. LSU, with its longtime relationship with the army, opted for its programs. Late in 1942, the school contracted with the U.S. government to operate an Army Administrative School training enlisted clerical and administrative personnel for the Army Air Corps. More than two thousand men completed the course during the six months of operation. Then in April 1943 came a Specialized Training and Reclassification unit (STAR), which screened up to one thousand men daily for possible ASTP assignment.

By mid-June 1943 LSU became one of 196 colleges to adopt the ASTP. The entire university switched that

August to the quarter system, placing itself on the ASTP schedule. During the 1943–44 school year, there were almost 1,700 trainees and 3,105 civilian students on campus.

How did the average civilian student fare during wartime at LSU? Forty years earlier, the student body had been 100 percent male. Now for the first time, it had a female majority. The remaining males, most subject to immediate draft, were cramming as many credit hours as possible before being called up for induction. Taking twenty hours was not uncommon. Little time remained for social activities.

Wartime brought on sacrifices. Goods such as gasoline, tires, automobiles, bicycles, typewriters, shoes, and many foods were rationed. As automobile usage dropped, most events moved to the campus or within walking distance. Dances were held in the Gym-Armory or the Field House, convocations in the Greek Theater. A few fraternities had houses, but sororities settled for their own rooms in the Panhellenic Building.

With casualties mounting overseas, the army desperately needed combat-ready troops. General George C. Marshall, chief of staff, presented the secretary of war with a choice: give him the men currently in the ASTP for the upcoming invasion or eliminate, in his planning for D-Day, ten divisions and twenty-nine anti-aircraft battalions. The secretary took the former route, virtually liquidating the entire ASTP. Effective

These dormitory presidents presided over meetings within their own residence halls and served on the central House Committee, which made the rules for all women living on campus. Listed from left to right are four of the eight: S. E. Cox; Louise Garig Hall; Nell Martin, Annie Boyd Hall; Martha "Gregor" Thompson, Highland Hall and chairman of the central House Committee; and Lily Volk, Grace King Hall. *Gumbo*, 1946.

Named for the heroine of Henry Wadsworth Longfellow's epic poem, Evangeline Hall serves as a women's residence hall.

March 1, 1944, all ASTP trainees at LSU were called into active duty except for advanced engineering and medical students. The terminated faculty members were paid through the end of the academic year.

Some trainees were accepted into Officer Candidate Schools (OCS). Others were in for a shock. Instead of attending OCS, they suddenly found themselves on the European front as privates, albeit the world's best-educated privates. Their immediate availability as trained troops, feel many analysts, was a key factor in the prompt defeat of the Nazis.

In May 1944, Louisianians inaugurated a new governor, James H. "Jimmie" Davis. A former Shreveport city commissioner, he was better known for his song

"You Are My Sunshine" than for politics. About this same time, Hodges suffered from a slight stroke and resigned the LSU presidency. He was replaced by William B. Hatcher, dean of the Junior Division and former school superintendent in East Baton Rouge Parish. Davis and Hatcher confronted a tremendous challenge in the face of declining army programs and the imminent arrival of large numbers of veterans.

In 1944 the GI Bill became law. Veterans serving ninety days or more would receive one year of education plus an additional period equal to total time in service. The maximum education allowed was four years.

By 1946 veterans received a monthly subsistence

Ready! Aim! Fire! In this 1940s-era photograph by Fonville Winans, four archers stand on a wall overlooking the Huey P. Long Swimming Pool. Considered risqué for its time period, this picture represents Winans's keen eye for detail and strong sense of artistic composition.

In this undated photograph, students marvel at the snow that covers the slope of the Indian Mounds. Jack Fiser Collection.

their textbooks, or the course of study pursued by each of their students. It simply paid the bills. GIs responded by the millions.

LSU was hard pressed to handle the record 8,705 GIs and other students who showed up for the fall 1946 semester. Classroom capacity was just one problem; there was also housing. Many male students were forced to stay in the old Army Air Corps barracks, several miles away at Harding Field (now Ryan Airport). Temporary facilities had to be erected along Nicholson Drive for married students.

The 1946 football season perked up returning GIs and eased the tensions of overcrowding. Quarterback Y. A. Tittle led the Tigers to a 9-1 record and the number eight spot in the Associated Press poll. The team then met Arkansas in the Cotton Bowl. But snow, ice, and frigid winds prevented either team from scoring a point.

By any measure, the GI Bill's educational benefits exceeded all expectations. Because of it, well over two million veterans attended college, and a grateful Louisiana and nation benefitted not only from their service during the war but by the well-educated body of citizens they became.

allowance of $65, if single, or $90 if married. The government would also pay $500 per school year for tuition, lodging, fees and books. At LSU, the general fee for the 1946–47 school year was $50, lodging was another $72, and books would run about $30. Other universities, even private ones, did not charge much more.

The GI Bill provided veterans with the opportunity to attend the college or university of their choice, public or private. It was the voucher system in its purest form. The federal government made no attempt to control the schools, their curriculum, their faculty,

"January 12—Toll of Tiger deaths in World War II hits a total of 211." *Gumbo*, 1945.

Quiet please. The students in
this 1931 photograph study
in Hill Memorial Library.

In 1902, sugar planter John
Hill, Sr., donated money to
LSU to construct a library in
memory of his son, John, Jr.
The younger Hill graduated
from LSU in 1873 and was
immediately appointed to
the Board of Supervisors by
Governor William Pitt Kellogg. He served on the board
until his death in 1893. Hill
Memorial Library became
its name on the new campus
in 1927. Over its history, Hill
has been home to the De-
partment of Architecture
and LSU Press. Today, it
houses LSU Libraries' Special Collections.

Students pose on the grand
stairway in Hill Memorial
Library. *Gumbo,* 1949.

Hill's facade. *Gumbo,* 1987

III THE RESEARCH UNIVERSITY

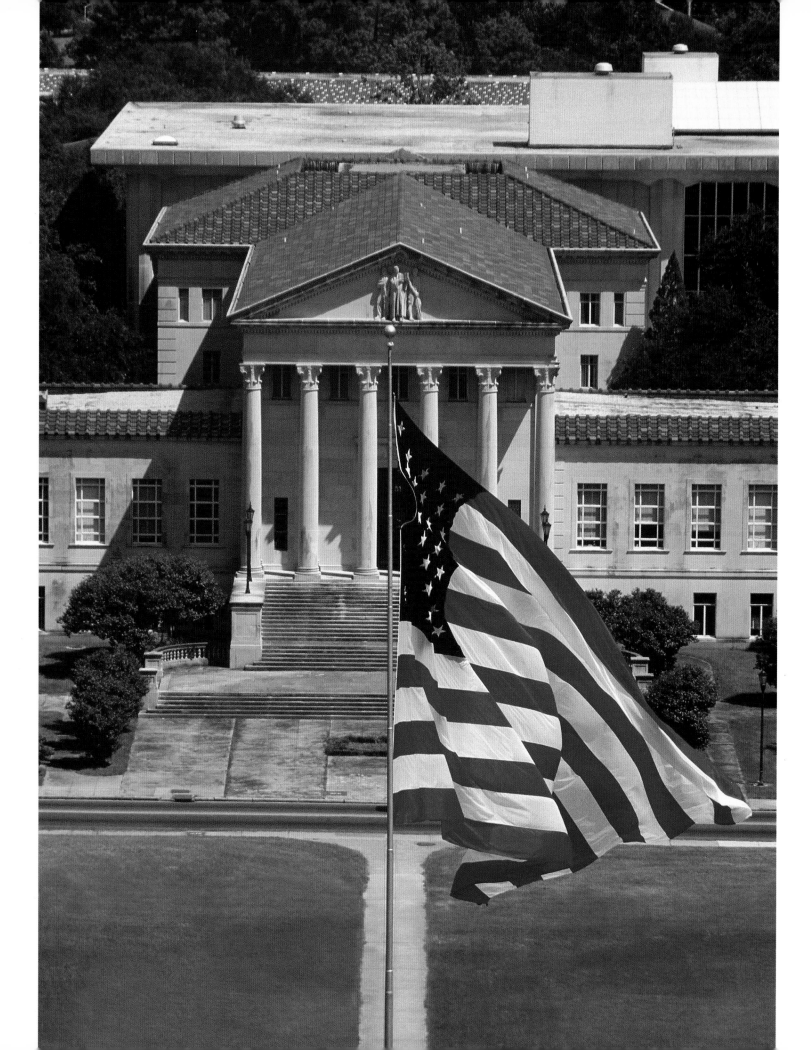

14   Postwar Progress

When President Hatcher's poor health forced him to retire in February 1947, the board named Fred C. Frey as acting president, and then conducted an exhaustive nationwide search to fill the post permanently. Board members wanted a well-known and widely respected educator, one who would improve the university's academic image and provide a stabilizing influence.

After reviewing 161 candidates, the board narrowed the list down to one: Harold W. Stoke, president of the University of New Hampshire, which, like LSU, was a land-grant institution as well as the state university. Before that, Stoke taught at the state universities of Nebraska, Tennessee, Pennsylvania, and Wisconsin. He also served as dean at two of those institutions. Stoke appeared to have the exact pedigree LSU wanted.

He received ten of the fourteen votes, decisive but not unanimous. LSU's comptroller, Troy H. Middleton, though not an applicant, garnered the remaining four.

To aid Stoke in his transition, acting president Fred C. Frey agreed to stay on his staff as dean of the university, and Troy H. Middleton remained comptroller. The following spring, the *Gumbo* commented, "[Stoke's] actions in regard to university policies have won him praise from every section. In his first year, he has done a remarkable job." This perhaps reflected the thoughts of most students and faculty. With such support, there seemed no way he could fail.

But Stoke had trouble relating to the board. He rarely spoke off the cuff, preferring to prepare written remarks and reading them verbatim at board meetings as well as most other occasions at which he had to speak.

Stoke also had his share of problems, including the Korean War and declining enrollment. By his second year, 1948–49, the student body had dipped slightly to 9,056—fledgling actress Joanne Woodward and 9,055

other students. And enrollment continued to fall to 5,664 by the time Stoke left.

Another concern was the junior colleges. Francis T. Nicholls in Thibodaux opened in September 1948 to become LSU's third junior college. Then in 1950 the trend reversed. Northeast and McNeese Junior College pulled way from LSU and soon became full universities

Wearing the "traditional" barrister's hat and cane, Law School officers Clarence E. Romero, president (left); Edwin W. Edwards, vice-president (center); and Virginia Martin, secretary-treasurer (right) pose for this photograph. *Gumbo,* 1949.

VANDY'S HEAD IN THE TIGER'S MOUTH

LSU tradition dictates that Greek organizations decorate their houses for homecoming games. In this 1947 photograph, the Delta Kappa Epsilon fraternity illustrates the popular cheer, "Eat 'em up, Tigers! Eat 'em up!" LSU defeated Vanderbilt 19-13. *Gumbo,* 1948.

under the State Board of Education (Nicholls Junior College left in 1956). Here the board's neglect was the primary culprit. The junior colleges simply became tired of life at the bottom of the food chain.

Even the football program fell into the doldrums. Yet life could be exciting, especially when the 1949 squad ran onto the field. Dubbed the "Cinderella Team," they unexpectedly knocked off the football giants, including three conference champions—North Carolina, Rice, and Tulane. They then had an opportunity to knock off a fourth, Oklahoma, in the Sugar Bowl on New Year's Day. When the clock struck twelve on New Year's Eve, however, the royal ball was over for Coach Gaynell Tinsley and his Cinderella Tigers. The next afternoon, LSU lost 35-0.

The Cinderella team's performance (and increased

attendance) prodded legislators into approving a bond issue for LSU to enlarge the stadium. This did not rank high on Stoke's priority list of needed capital improvements. Happily for him, a lackluster 1950 season removed some of the pressure. In any case, the federal government put a halt to all unessential construction for the duration of the Korean conflict.

On December 28, 1950, Stoke shocked the university community by requesting a special board meeting to consider his resignation. The board met and his resignation was accepted after a lengthy discussion. Apparently friction between Stoke and the board had been developing for some time. Stoke's formality and rigid dialog did not go over well with some board members. But there were deeper problems. Stoke antagonized people when he tried to block construction of a new

WAR MEMORIALS ON CAMPUS

The Campanile, the campus's signature structure, initially known as the Soldiers' and Sailors' Memorial, was dedicated on April 30, 1926, in a ceremony separate from the main dedication of the new campus. Underwritten by the American Legion, the Campanile honors the 1,500 Louisianians who lost their lives during World War I. In 1928 the Legislature appropriated $10,000 for the bronze tablets placed inside the tower listing the state's departed servicemen by parish. Somehow Pointe Coupee parish and its fourteen dead were left off.

Of that 1,500, the thirty (some records say thirty-one) LSU students and alumni were each remembered with a live oak planted in the Memorial Grove located on Highland Road just south of the Parade Ground.

During the mid-1990s, the Alumni Association solicited contributions to update the memorials—to honor those LSU students, faculty, alumni, and staff killed or reported missing in action during World War II and subsequent military conflicts. The efforts of the Association resulted in a War Memorial Commission, which constructed a new monument on the Parade Ground adjacent to the flagpole. Here, etched in granite, are the names of 624 fallen Tigers. Former president George H. W. Bush helped to dedicate the site in ceremonies held on October 8, 1998.

The next project of the War Memorial Commission is renovating the Campanile to house the long-awaited LSU Military Museum.

LSU researcher St. John Poindexter Chilton and an unidentified U.S. Department of Agriculture official examine the first flowering canes at the Sugar Experiment Station. In 1949, Chilton and his associate Clayton C. Moorland (not pictured) perfected photoperiod control, a technique that forces sugarcane to flower by artificially altering the length of the day. Because Louisiana is further north than other sugar-producing regions, cane does not flower naturally here. Forced flowering allows researchers to cross pollinate different varieties of sugarcane and to produce disease resistant and more productive hybrids. Scientists at the Sugar Experiment Station, which merged with the Audubon Sugar Institute in 1988, also conduct research in pest management and look for uses for sugar industry by-products.

Lab School. He also irritated a large bloc of the campus community by trying to remove all religious centers from the campus.

Some felt LSU would suffer permanent damage from this resignation, but they were wrong. The university had an uncanny knack of bouncing back. At that same meeting in December, board members moved swiftly to name Stoke's replacement. There would be no long search, not even a short one. This time, they knew whom they wanted—General Troy H. Middleton, the comptroller.

Except for a one-year tour of duty in the Philippines and his service during World War II, Middleton had been at LSU since 1930. He had filled a number of

1948

LSU's third junior college, Francis T. Nicholls, opens in Thibodaux.

1950

McNeese and Northeast junior colleges pull away from LSU to join the State Board of Education. LSU enrolls first black student into Law School.

roles—ROTC commandant, dean, and comptroller. The supervisors knew his skills and his ability to delegate authority.

Middleton inherited his share of problems, the major one being how to use the funds allocated for enlarging the football stadium. The money, though available, could not be used for a non-essential structure during wartime. Middleton preferred using the money for a library, then going back to the legislature later for the stadium enlargement. Meanwhile, the student council entered the picture with a strong preference for a new auditorium over the other two projects. Governor Earl K. Long agreed to come up with an additional appropriation, which when used with the stadium money, could build both the library and auditorium instead. But athletic director T. P. Heard stayed a step ahead of them, successfully lobbying the legislature and the board to leave stadium funds intact even though they could not then be used.

As the library plan began to pick up momentum, the legislature discussed ditching it for other proposed projects. A patient Middleton kept up the pressure for the library and the auditorium. But closing the oval in

About one-tenth the size of an industrial sugar factory, the Audubon Experimental Factory is the ideal size for instruction and experimentation. In this photograph, a crane removes sugarcane from a truck. *Gumbo,* 1949.

These men feed sugarcane into an automatic stripper.

1956

Mike the Tiger dies and is replaced by Mike II, who promptly dies in his sleep. Second Mike II secretly replaces the first, who is supposedly undergoing treatment at the Audubon Park Zoo.

1956

Nicholls Junior College leaves LSU.

1957

LSU alumna Joanne Woodward wins an Oscar for best actress for her role in *The Three Faces of Eve.*

1958

LSU opens the integrated four-year school LSU–New Orleans (now University of New Orleans).

Tiger Stadium came first. For years, fans referred to the new south end as the "library section."

Middleton ultimately prevailed in the case of the other two projects. In 1958 a new two-story library opened. Fortunately, Middleton insisted on a founda-

tion that could accommodate a four-floor structure. The two extra floors soon became necessary, and would be completed in 1974. Other locations were available, but Middleton held out for a spot in the middle of a quadrangle, where the students could find it. The library is convenient, but it blocks a formerly panoramic view of the quadrangle from Atkinson Hall to Foster Hall.

In 1958, the LSU football team became the national champions for the first and only time to date. Coach Gaynell "Gus" Tinsley, though well liked, had a dismal record. Following the 1954 season, the board decided to buy up the remaining two years of Tinsley's contract (at $12,500 a year) and to retire athletic director T. P. Heard. After an extensive search, they hired Paul Dietzel away from West Point as LSU's new head coach. This turned out to be an excellent move. It took him a season or two, but Dietzel turned the program completely around.

Also in 1958, Louisiana State University in New Orleans opened, becoming a source of pride to Middleton. LSU leased a 178-acre lakefront site where a naval air station had stood. The conditions were affordable: a ninety-nine-year lease for a dollar a year. The site included a number of buildings that were readily

Construction of Middleton Library. Crews excavate a large area of the Quadrangle between Memorial Tower and Hill Memorial Library. *Gumbo,* 1957.

convertible into temporary classrooms. LSUNO opened with just under fifteen hundred students. Renamed the University of New Orleans but still in the LSU system, it has since become a major university in its own right.

The desegregation fight approached its peak during Middleton's tenure. LSU had been all-white since opening day 1860. The separate-but-equal doctrine was still the law of the land, and LSU preferred to keep it that way. School policy dictated that blacks be admitted only through legislation or court order. This occurred first on the graduate level—where Southern University had no comparable offerings.

LSU's first black student, Roy S. Wilson, enrolled in the Law School during the fall of 1950, just months before Middleton assumed the reins. Several hundred more black students matriculated on the graduate level during the 1950s.

The LSU board acquiesced to a 1958 court order to integrate the New Orleans campus. Yet it continued its legal battles to delay integration in its Baton Rouge undergraduate program until 1964. Once under way, however, the transition proceeded smoothly. By 1972,

Before the campus began to expand outward, students going to or from their classes were forced to walk by Middleton Library. Note that in this photograph, ca. 1959, the library only has two floors. The third and fourth floors were added in the mid-1970s.

Founded in 1960, the International Club gave all students a chance to learn about the customs of the countries that make up the LSU community. This dance, ca. 1964, was part of a festival sponsored by the club. Today's international students enjoy the International Cultural Center on Dalrymple Drive.

1960

LSU opens new junior college, LSU at Alexandria, at its Dean Lee Agricultural Center.

1962

Campus-wide self-study leads to "Centers of Excellence" grants from the National Science Foundation.

109

The pictured candidates for student government along with their supporters campaign in front of the Field House.

After a rare snowfall in February 1960, these coeds build a snowman in the Quadrangle. Atkinson Hall is visible in the background. *Gumbo,* 1960.

Coeds walk up the steps of the new Student Union, which was dedicated in 1964. Located at the approximate geographic center of campus, the Union meets the cultural and social needs of students and faculty members.

This convocation, held in Parker Coliseum, was one of the many events held to celebrate LSU's centennial. *Gumbo,* 1960.

LSU had a black president of the student body, Kerry Pourciau.

When Middleton reached the mandatory retirement age of seventy in 1959, the board asked him to stay on. He finally retired in February 1962 with an enviable record. New buildings had been built. Old buildings had been renovated. Enrollment passed the ten thousand mark for the first time. In fact, it had doubled during the general's tenure. Middleton led LSU through a period of unprecedented growth. More than that, he placed the university back on track, focusing on its future.

The practice of head shaving continued until the late 1960s. This 1966 photograph shows a new crop of cadets undergoing orientation. In 1968 the Board of Supervisors voted, after being lobbied by students and faculty members, to end compulsory military training thus ending a tradition that had lasted for over a century.

Commencement in Parker Coliseum, 1967.

LSU football team, 1897. Playing only two games that year, the Tigers held a season record of 1-1. The previous season the university adopted the nickname "Tigers" after Coach Allen W. Jeardeau led his team to a 6-0 season.

The 1903 football team finished the season with a record of 4–5.

LSU football great Dalton Hilliard (pictured scoring a touchdown) was the team's rushing leader from 1982 to 1985, was scoring leader in his junior and senior years, and was named the Offensive MVP in 1984 and in 1985. Photograph courtesy LSU Sports Information.

LSU's rivalry with the Tulane Green Wave was a natural one because of the proximity of the two schools. The Greenies won LSU's first-ever football game by the score of 34–0. In this 1922 photograph, an LSU student kneels in mock grief at the Tulane Goat Grave. That year, LSU defeated its main rival by a score of 25–14.

WANTED!

"THE HUSTLERS"

THE HUSTLERS ARE: (sitting, left to right) "SMARTY" Marty Allman, Mike "BIG MAC" Darnall, Jeff "POGO" Taylor, Dawn "HOLLYWOOD SUNSET" Tonkovich, Wade "RED MAN" Evans, "OUTBACK" Eddie Palubinskas, and "DANDY" Rarely Herring. Standing (from left:) John "THE ROOKIE" Enquist, Rick "WOLF" Walters, "BABY-FACE" Carl Siener, Ralph "THE MISSISSIPPI GAMBLER" Loe, "FAST" Eddie Le Blanc, Collis "THE KENTWOOD KID!" Temple, and "WILD" Bill Whittle. Missing from picture: "CRYSTAL" Chris Raymond.

DESCRIPTION: A band of energetic young athletes with great ideals . . . they have unreal goals . . . they are armed with desire, unity, hustle, defense, conditioning, guts, hearts, and a winning attitude . . . THEY ARE WELL COACHED . . .

WANTED IN THE FOLLOWING STATES . . . UTAH: for beating one of the nation's winningest basketball teams in the NCAA over the past ten years, WEBER STATE . . . TENNESSEE: for assault and battery on MEMPHIS STATE'S hopes of an unbeaten and nationally ranked season and dreams of a national championship and for giving VANDERBILT fits . . . . FLORIDA: for shooting down the GATORS and robbing all but four of them of any points at all . . . ALABAMA: for handing nationally ranked 'BAMA one of its stiffest battles at home in years and for driving AUBURN crazy . . . MEXICO: for beating the University of America's, and under internationa rules, too . . . THERE WILL BE MORE BEFORE THE SEASON IS OVER!!

COURT will be held in the LSU Assembly Center and 14,351 jurors are needed to try the cases . . . AGAINST KENTUCKY (Jan. 27), TENNESSEE (Jan. 29), ALABAMA (Feb. 10) AUBURN (Feb. 12), TULANE (Feb. 14), MISSISSIPPI STATE (Mar. 1), and OLE MISS (Mar. 3).

THE HUSTLERS HAVE HOPES OF BREAKING THE ALL-TIME LSU AND STATE OF LOUISIANA ATTENDANCE RECORDS FOR BASKETBALL COURT CASES . . . . THE RECORD IS 11,500 AT LSU AND 13,200 FOR THE STATE.

--YOU BE THE JUDGE--
BEWARE: THESE GUYS WILL STEAL YOUR HEARTS!

Dale Brown coached this team of "hustlers" (above) during the 1973–74 season. On the back row, number 41, Collis Temple, Jr., became the first black basketball player at LSU. Collis Temple III played his freshman season under LSU Tigers' coach John Brady in 1998. *Gumbo,* 1973.

In this 1975 action, LSU tries to block a Florida shot. During the 1980s, the Tigers went on to appear in two NCAA Final Four tournaments. *Gumbo,* 1975.

Pete Maravich came to LSU with his father, head basketball coach Press Maravich. Young Maravich played for LSU from 1968 to 1970 and was named Associated Press collegiate player of the year each season. Nicknamed "Pistol" Pete because of his shooting style, he scored 3,667 points and averaged 44.2 points per game. Maravich moved on to the pros, where in 1987, he entered the National Basketball Association's Hall of Fame. He died of a heart attack, January 5, 1998, in Pasadena, California, at the age of 40. Photograph courtesy LSU Sports Information.

On Hallowe'en night, 1959, Billy Cannon, became an LSU legend when he returned a punt eighty-nine yards for a game-winning touchdown over the Ole Miss Rebels. He won the coveted Heisman Trophy in 1959. He is the only LSU football player to be so honored. Photograph courtesy LSU Sports Information.

In the 1996 College World Series, Warren Morris stepped up to the plate in the bottom of the ninth inning with two outs, a runner on, and LSU trailing Miami 8-7. As fans held their breath, he hit the first pitch out of the park for 9-8 Tiger victory and the college national championship. Under Coach Stanley "Skip" Bertman, the Tiger baseball team has won the College World Series five times—in 1991, 1993, 1996, 1997, and 2000. Photograph courtesy LSU Sports Information.

Gumbo, 1983.

Katrina Hibbert, from Melbourne, Australia, a member of the Lady Tigers Basketball Team, fights for the basket in a game against Tennessee's Lady Vols. This basket late in the game allowed LSU to defeat the number-one-ranked Tennessee by a score of 72-69 in 1999. Photograph courtesy LSU Sports Information.

Performing a dismount from the balance beam, a member of LSU's gymnastics team concludes her routine. Photograph courtesy LSU Sports Information.

The Lady Tigers dominate the sport of track and field winning twelve national titles between 1987 and 2000. Peta-Gaye Dowdie (center), from Spanishtown, Jamaica, competes in both the 100-meter and 200-meter distances. Photograph courtesy LSU Sports Information.

After a sixteen-year absence, softball returned to LSU in 1997. In 2000, the Lady Tigers won their first SEC-West title. Ashley Ducote, shown here reaching for home plate, contributed to her team's success. Photograph courtesy LSU Sports Information.

15   The Quest for Excellence

In February 1962, the board named John A. Hunter as Middleton's successor. He had a well-rounded background at LSU, having served as registrar, dean of the Junior Division, and dean of Student Services. Under his leadership, LSU continued to grow, passing fifteen thousand in enrollment in the fall of 1964. This was in addition to LSUNO, the Medical School, and a new junior college (LSU at Alexandria, established in 1960).

LSU had become unwieldy. One president running the Baton Rouge campus on a day-to-day basis must also supervise the Alexandria and New Orleans campuses.

A growing threat was the State Board of Education, which in addition to elementary and secondary education, operated all of the other state colleges in Louisiana, including the three that were originally junior-college branches of LSU. As the board began

Photographer David Gleason climbed to the top of the Memorial Tower to shoot this mid-1960s picture of the cadet corps drilling on the Parade Ground. The Law School is visible in the background. David Gleason Photograph Collection.

1964	1965	1965
First African American students successfully enroll in LSU's undergraduate program.	First chancellor appointed for Baton Rouge campus, leading to a new LSU System.	Hubert H. Humphrey (M.A. '40) inaugurated as vice-president of the United States.

upgrading the colleges into universities complete with graduate programs, LSU's role as the state's comprehensive university appeared in jeopardy.

Meeting this challenge required greater flexibility. Hunter responded by slowly relinquishing control of the Baton Rouge campus. On February 6, 1965, he named his arts and sciences dean, Cecil G. "Pete" Taylor, to the new position of chancellor. Hunter remained as president overall, but the Baton Rouge deans began reporting to Taylor.

Although this date marks the unofficial beginning of the LSU System, it was strictly that—the beginning. The transfer of power came in gradual steps over a period of years. With the new chancellor proving his

Compare the size of these early computers with today's desktop, laptop, and hand-held varieties.

In the fall of 1963, the parking problems that had long plagued the university grew worse as enrollment increased and the number of students driving their own vehicles to campus rose. To counter that problem, officials created the Tiger Train (pictured above) to transport students to the center of campus from the outlying parking lots. Painted purple and gold with a tiger head on the first car, these trains ran until 1970.

Practice makes perfect! The concert band rehearses for an upcoming performance. *Gumbo*, 1965.

1966
Two new junior colleges open— LSU at Eunice and LSU in Shreveport.

1967
Hubert H. Humphrey is Democratic candidate for U.S. president. Veterinary School opens.

mettle in Baton Rouge, other campuses also followed suit with decentralization and selection of their own chancellors, including the campuses established during the 1960s—LSU in Shreveport, LSU at Eunice, and a new medical school in Shreveport.

LSU offers courses to help its international students become proficient speakers and writers of the English language. Here, a small group of international students hone their skills with the help of their instructor. Photographs, ca. 1965.

This transfer of power was fortuitous. Creation of the LSU System reflected an unprecedented demand for higher education as the leading edge of the "baby-boom" generation reached college age. LSU's initial response to burgeoning enrollment was to build more dormitories and new dining halls; to renovate the Student Health Center; and to authorize the building of sorority houses. The new Student Union, completed in 1964, fit with this effort to continue collegiate traditions established in the interwar period. But by the end of the 1960s, the attempt to maintain a residential college and the *in loco parentis* (in place of parents) restrictions on students, especially women, had collapsed. Gone were the dress codes and dorm closing hours. Gone too was mandatory ROTC for freshman and sophomore men; it was made voluntary in 1969. Students flocked to the apartment complexes that sprang up off Nicholson Drive. The stadium dorms closed, to eventually be followed by the men's dorms (Johnston, Hatcher, and others) built in the 1950s. Women became a majority of students in the late 1990s.

With the desegregation of LSU's undergraduate programs in 1964, new friendships were forged . . .

. . . and old friendships retained. Photographs ca. 1970.

Freshman dance, ca. 1966.

The "baby-boom" students not only resisted the old rules, some of them also supported racial integration and the anti–Vietnam War movement. Free Speech Alley in front of the Union rang with impassioned speech and saw demonstrations on these issues of the day. Students "sat in" the offices of the Dean of Students and the Chancellor. Students participated in marches and other demonstrations. Meanwhile in the courts, LSU continued to resist desegregation of its undergraduate programs until ordered to admit African American students without restrictions in 1964. It was at least another decade before black students had more

Founded in November 1964, Free Speech Alley provides students with a forum to discuss a wide variety of topics including politics (above right), social issues, and religion (above). Debates often become heated as people with opposing views express their opinions. However, the spirit of fair play still prevails at the Alley, and anyone who wants to speak is given the opportunity. Free Speech Alley has undergone renovations to provide stadium seating and other improvements. Gumbo, 1966.

1968
Second Medical School reopens, this one in Shreveport.

1970
T. Harry Williams wins Pulitzer Prize for his biography, Huey Long.

than a token presence on what was for a long time after 1964 a hostile campus, however welcoming some students were.

Troubling as these events were for some LSU officials, alumni, and Louisiana residents, the campus unrest was mild compared to what happened at some universities. The lowering of the age of majority to eighteen and the granting of the right to vote were among the fruits of this nationwide student agitation.

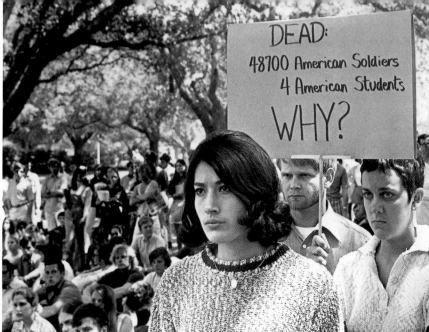

Chancellor Cecil "Pete" Taylor listens intently to the opinions of this masked antiwar demonstrator.

Coinciding with the baby-boom enrollment surge was the further development of LSU's research activities. A campuswide self-study in 1962–63 launched this new emphasis. An early result was the success of faculty in the departments of chemistry, physics and astronomy, mathematics, and geology in obtaining a Centers of Excellence grant from the National Science Foundation. By the end of the 1960s LSU, long known

LSU student Luana Henderson takes part in a peaceful anti–Vietnam War demonstration on the LSU campus. The poster behind her refers to the killing on May 4, 1970, of four students by National Guardsmen during an antiwar protest on the campus of Kent State University in Ohio.

LSU student Leo Hamilton (pictured with bullhorn) leads a protest against the November 1972 shooting deaths of two Southern University students by the police. *Gumbo*, 1974.

Before the days of REGGIE, LSU's touch-tone phone registration system, students stood in long lines in the Assembly Center to schedule their courses. Photograph ca. 1969.

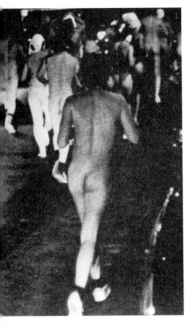

Taking part in a national fad of the early 1970s, male students streak down sorority row. *Gumbo,* 1974.

for its work in agriculture and chemistry, began to attain recognition in other sciences and even the humanities. T. Harry Williams won the Pulitzer Prize for his biography of Huey Long in 1970.

With the Centers of Excellence funding as a base, LSU faculty in the sciences rapidly expanded their grant writing and research programs. This activity soon created a need for more laboratories, especially in chemistry and the life sciences. The eventual result was the construction of such facilities as Williams Hall and Choppin Hall in the 1970s. Expansion of research facilities continues, inevitably lagging behind opportunities and faculty ambitions.

Martin D. Woodin replaced John A. Hunter as president in 1972. By the time Taylor announced his retirement two years later, the concept of a separate chancellor was well established—so much so that the university tried a rarely used approach in seeking his replacement. The school created a search committee (which has since become standard procedure) to find the best-qualified person for the job. The committee's choice was Paul W. Murrill, provost and vice-chancellor for academic affairs.

Almost immediately, Murrill's and Woodin's future and the university's were in jeopardy. A constitutional convention, then in session, leaned toward use of a

single Board of Regents with direct control over all state universities, including LSU. Led by Woodin and Murrill, Tiger faithful fought back. When voters approved the new state constitution in late 1974, they could choose between two concepts of higher education governance: Proposition A, three management boards (including the LSU supervisors) and a supervisory board; or Proposition B, just one board.

When votes were counted, proposition A was ratified by a higher percentage (62 percent) than was the

Students become the teacher in this 1972 social welfare class.

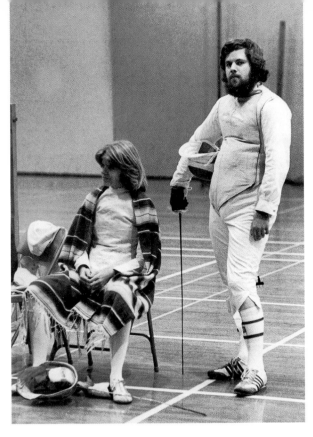

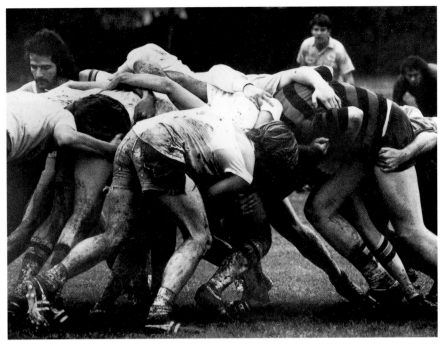

An intramural rugby team practices on the Parade Ground, 1974.

Members of the Fencing Club, Cat Davis and Ben Price, watch one of their teammates take the strip at a 1972 tournament. The Fencing Club, which was founded in the late nineteenth century, is one of the oldest clubs in existence at LSU. Photograph courtesy of Dr. Benjamin L. Price.

constitution itself (58 percent). For the first time, the System as a legal entity had constitutional sanction.

The Baton Rouge campus (officially now Louisiana State University and Agricultural and Mechanical College) of LSU became an autonomous unit of that system, a transition with many challenges. Murrill

The Huey P. Long Swimming Pool.

Mike the Mascot and the cheerleaders in front of the Assembly Center, ca. 1974.

This baby tiger accompanies her father to a 1973 football game. GO TIGERS!

Researchers conduct experiments in a Choppin Hall chemistry laboratory, 1977.

Choppin Hall, 1975. The Chemistry Department moved from the Charles Edward Coates Chemical Laboratories building, which was constructed in 1925, to its current location. This seven-story building is named for Arthur R. Choppin, a former dean of the college.

continued to build the students, staff, faculty, alumni, and other friends into a cohesive university community working toward a common goal—to lift LSU to the top 1 percent of the nation's more than three thousand colleges and universities.

This was a tall order, considering LSU still had an open admission policy, swelling enrollment, and consequent overcrowding. The core campus, the quadrangles, were designed for a maximum of five thousand. By this time, there were four times that many. And the quadrangles were not expandable. Relief could only come from new construction away from the core.

The School of Veterinary Science, for example, shared space in eight buildings before moving to its present building on the River Road in 1978. Likewise, space constraints for the Center for Engineering and Business Administration were solved when CEBA opened its new building on the south side of campus two years later.

Thanks to an improved state economy, construction flourished on the Baton Rouge campus under Murrill and on the other LSU campuses under Woodin. Funds likewise became available for a multitude of new programs. It was an era of great gains.

In 1795, planter Étienne de Boré revolutionized Louisiana's sugar industry by successfully granulating sugar in commercial quantities, first using this sugar kettle on his plantation near New Orleans. Currently, the kettle rests beside the Chemical Engineering Building.

Members of Alpha Zeta, an honors fraternity for agriculture majors, pose in front of Parker Coliseum, ca. 1975. *Gumbo.*

Bo Blackmun studies shrimp migration, 1970. Photograph courtesy Sea Grant College.

Dr. James G. Gosselink, from the Sea Grant College, used this houseboat to conduct a primary productivity study. He tested the instruments on land before taking them into the marsh, August 1975. Photograph courtesy Sea Grant College.

Completed in 1976, Kirby Smith Hall was named in honor of Confederate general Edmund Kirby Smith. This thirteen-story, air-conditioned dormitory was built to house 734 male students. It is located behind the Pentagon dormitories.

1972

1972

LSU in Shreveport becomes a four-year institution.

The Agricultural Center established as a separate entity.

Noted historian and Pulitzer Prize winner T. Harry Williams captivated students with his dynamic lectures. His Civil War course was one of the most popular classes taught on campus, and students who were not enrolled in it would often line up outside of his classroom just to hear his lectures. Williams is shown here lecturing to a packed house, 1975.

The Center for Engineering and Business Administration, better known as CEBA, was completed in 1978 at a cost of $15 million.

Leaning over her pottery wheel, this student shapes her piece of art.

Progress came in other areas as well. In 1978, LSU became the thirteenth institution to be granted sea-grant status. The land-grant act of the 1860s emphasized the proper harvesting of land. The sea-grant act of 1966, in turn, emphasized the harvesting of lakes and oceans, many already overfished. LSU also remains a leader in its study of coastal ecosystems and wetlands restoration.

Murrill stepped down in 1981, replaced by an interim chancellor, Otis B. Wheeler, who continued the momentum until the new chancellor, James H. Wharton, dean of the University College, assumed command. Wharton renewed LSU's pursuit of excellence, underscoring the need for stronger graduate education with emphasis on research.

LSU's efforts paid dividends. The university received initial funding for its synchrotron, around which the present J. Bennett Johnston, Sr., Center for Advanced Microstructures and Devices (CAMD) developed. As one of eight such centers in the United States, CAMD provides basic research in atomic and molecular structure as well as applied research in microdevice fabrication. In 1987, the Carnegie Foundation designated LSU a Research I institution—its highest category, shared with only sixty-nine other schools.

Enrollment first topped thirty thousand in 1982. Two years later, Wharton, recognizing that growth alone does not bring quality, made a daring move. He persuaded the board to adopt admission standards for the first time. Many viewed the move as reckless and almost suicidal. Once the standards became effective

1974

New state constitution approved. LSU System becomes a legal entity for the first time. Also creates the Southern University System.

1974

All other institutions of higher education placed under new board of trustees (currently referred to as the University of Louisiana System). All boards report to a new board of regents.

LSU's status as a research institution provides opportunities for students and faculty to advance the larger body of knowledge and to challenge older ways of examining the environment. Here a scientist uses an electron microscope.

Civil Engineering class, late 1970s.

No longer only a sponsor. By 1976, female students not only joined ROTC, they also became officers.

1977

The Law Center becomes a separate campus under the LSU System.

1978

LSU is designated a sea-grant institution.

1978

The School of Veterinary Science moves to its present river front location.

In 1985, LSU's Ballet Corps and majorettes combined to form the Golden Girls. This Golden Girl prepares to take the field.

Chancellor Paul Murrill discusses issues important to students on the LSU campus. Photograph 1980.

(in 1988), enrollment did drop—though never below twenty-five thousand.

At the same time, LSU faced its first major financial crisis since World War II. The problem was the state's dependence on petroleum—from severance tax collection to production on state-owned lands. When oil prices dropped over 50 percent during the 1980s, it created havoc with Louisiana's finances. The university found its state funding cut year after year. In some years, it was trimmed a second time—after the school had already committed the money. LSU reduced expenses by pruning nonessential programs and personnel, raising tuition and fees, and postponing maintenance. The Athletic Department even donated part of its surplus to slow the hemorrhaging. But the cuts kept coming, forcing the elimination of some crucial degree programs. Finances remained tight until oil prices slowly began improving in the late 1980s

When Wharton stepped down in 1989, the board brought in E. Grady Bogue, chancellor at LSU in Shreveport, as interim chancellor. He already knew the people and understood the system. Hence the transi-

Students rush to get out of the rain during "Jam-Jam" on South Stadium Drive, 1979.

tion turned out to be quite smooth, especially with the easing of the money crunch.

William E. "Bud" Davis, who replaced Bogue, came to LSU from the Oregon higher education system later in 1989, determined to make the campus a more student-friendly one. The honors program attained "college" status in 1992. That same year, the successful Student Recreational Sports Complex, funded by self-

Alumni Association president Tom Ruffin and Governor David C. Treen crown the 1980 homecoming queen, Elissa Gomez.

imposed student fees, opened its doors. And a cultural center for African American students was established.

Davis never lost sight of LSU's research objectives. In 1992, LSU received the first federal funding for its Center for Coastal Energy and Environmental Resources, since renamed the School of the Coast and Environment, soon to occupy a new complex on Nicholson Drive. Fundraising activities ensued. Three former presidents—Jimmy Carter, Gerald Ford, and

The LSU Bookstore has always been one of the busiest spots on campus at the beginning of each semester. The Union now houses a Barnes & Noble bookstore to serve the campus.

In 1982 the Departments of Agronomy and Anthropology discovered that LSU's Indian Mounds are more than five thousand years old. The scientists pictured here took six core samples to help determine the age of the mounds.

In April 1981, a fire broke out in Peabody Hall, which was one of the original buildings on the new campus, and destroyed its top floor. The fire caused approximately $1 million in damages. This photograph shows an early phase of reconstruction. Peabody is currently the headquarters for the College of Education. *Gumbo,* 1981.

George H. W. Bush—helped dedicate the Lod Cook Alumni Center in 1994. The following year, the LSU Foundation initiated an ambitious six-year "LSU Campaign" to raise $150 million.

Davis resigned in 1996, becoming a tenured professor in education. With a scholarship crisis in the making, the board decided to by-pass the national search and move directly to the selection process. Their choice: William L. Jenkins, LSU provost, former dean of the Veterinary School, and a native of South Africa. Employing input from the faculty and staff, he redefined LSU's goals and developed a strategic plan to lead LSU into the twenty-first century. Jenkins worked closely with the LSU Campaign to develop a permanent endowment. A vigorous response soon justified increasing the goal to $225 million in 1997. Another of the many tasks he oversaw was increased and long-overdue maintenance.

Allen A. Copping, system president, retired in 1999 after fourteen years. One of his major feats was to bring the Pennington Biomedical Research Center to Baton Rouge. He was succeeded by Jenkins that same

year, which made Jenkins the first chancellor to also serve as president.

Mark A. Emmert, president of the University of Connecticut, another land-grant institution, assumed the role of LSU's chancellor in 1999. His goal is straightforward. He sees LSU as a leading research university, taking students to the highest level of intellectual and personal development. The university is not yet where he wants it, but is moving up fast. Toward

Study or leisure? This student takes a multidirectional approach to learning.

1981

John Kennedy Toole receives Pulitzer Prize posthumously for his novel, *A Confederacy of Dunces,* published by LSU Press.

1981

Mike III escapes from cage one night, setting off frantic campus-wide search. Thanks to tranquilizer darts, he is recaptured before any harm is done.

Sorority sisters forever! Photograph ca. 1981.

Unable to decide whether to watch the big game or spend the afternoon basking in the Louisiana sunshine, these fraternity brothers decide to do both. Photograph ca. 1980.

As the semester draws to a close, students living in residence halls pack up their belongings and return home.

this end, admission standards are to be tightened again in 2002, and the already excellent honors program is being expanded.

The university will have a larger budget to oversee. Higher oil prices combined with a supportive governor and legislature are helping LSU to catch up—on over-due pay raises, course offerings, and some remaining delayed maintenance. Elise Grenier, a specialist in art restoration, began restoring the Allen Hall frescoes designed by Conrad Albrizio. Better funding likewise meant new capital outlays as well as upgraded research facilities.

Even more exciting was Governor M. J. "Mike" Foster's Information Technology Initiative. Leading the way will be LSU and its Center for Applied Information Technology and Learning (or LSU Capital). The state's investment in information technology (IT) represents a godsend for LSU, putting it on the cutting edge in research—and giving the university a head start over peer institutions, many of which face declining support. In addition to helping the school, it will stimulate the state's economic development.

The six-year LSU Campaign closed its books on June 30, 2001, after raising $255 million, primarily in gifts restricted to specific schools or projects such as Paula Garvey Manship's contributions to kick off a fund-raising campaign for LSU's new downtown art museum, as well as a new organ pavilion for the School of Music and the campus community.

LSU students continued to take high honors in many ways. Their *Legacy* magazine—which first appeared in 1993—was designated by the Society of Professional Journalists in 2001 as the "best [collegiate] magazine published more than once a year."

One 2001 highlight was Elizabeth Dole's keynote speech at the "Under the Arches" program commemo-

1986

Constitutional amendment preserves a large portion of 8(g) funds for endowed professorships and chairs.

1987

Carnegie Foundation ranks LSU as a Research I Institution (its highest category).

1988

LSU initiates admission standards for first time.

rating the Diamond Jubilee anniversary of the dedication of the present campus. The year's events presented the ideal time to step back and take stock. Just how far has LSU come since that first 1925–26 school year on its present campus?

Compared to the not-yet-completed quadrangle in 1925, today's LSU boasts 250 major buildings. Most have been completed since World War II. The buildings, lakes, and landscaping create an environment which is, as Thomas A. Gaines expresses in *The Campus as a Work of Art,* "a botanical joy to behold at any time of the year." He ranks LSU as the number eleven campus in the country. The university will hold or better that ranking; it recently engaged Smith Group JJR to develop a comprehensive master plan for the campus with broad-based faculty, student, and public involvement.

There are now nine senior colleges, three schools,

Unidentified sorority sisters decorate their house for homecoming, ca. 1984.

Members of the Tiger Band take a break from practice. Photograph ca. 1984.

and over eighty-five research centers, labs, institutes, and programs. To support them are three million volumes, and still counting, in the LSU libraries.

In athletics, football is still king. Additions to Tiger Stadium since 1926 have increased its capacity from 12,000 to 91,600, the nation's fifth largest. In other sports, Tigers reign as well. In 2000, LSU's baseball team won the College World Series for the fifth time since 1991, and basketball also continues to draw crowds. But athletes are likewise excelling in what were once considered minor sports. For example, in 2000 also, the women's track team won its twelfth national championship. LSU's Meredith Duncan won the 2001 U.S. Women's Amateur golf title. And a former Tiger golfer, David Toms, squeezed out a close victory in the Professional Golfers Association (PGA) Tournament.

Now LSU has seventeen hundred full-time professors and other faculty members. In addition to the new IT program and the new positions it will provide, LSU continues to take advantage of the so-called "8(g)" funds derived through a settlement between Louisiana and the federal government over disputed off-shore oil and gas revenue. Administered by the Board of Re-

1992

The Honors program attains "college" status.

1995

The LSU Campaign begins; raises $255 million in next six years.

The Division of Continuing Education, an outgrowth of the Hatch Act of 1887, sponsors programs ranging from independent study for individuals to counterterrorist education courses for municipal, state, and federal workers. Firefighter's Training (the Fire and Emergency Training Institute) is one of the department's oldest and most renowned programs. In this group of photographs, which were taken in the 1970s, firemen hone their skills.

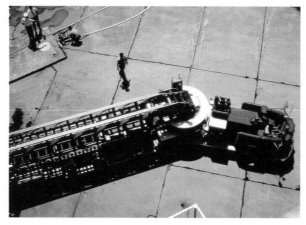

gents, the plan provides for $100,000 endowed professorships and $1,000,000 endowed chairs, where private sources contribute 60 percent of the money and the 8(g) program funds the balance. Through August 2001, LSU (including the Law and Agricultural Centers) has been awarded 341 endowed professorships (31 percent of the state's total) and 42 endowed chairs (21 percent). And the university is working aggressively to increase that number, to attract and retain the very best faculty.

No discussion of the faculty would be complete without emphasizing the importance of the currently more than three thousand staff members and their

Students wait to have their fee bills checked and stamped. Photograph ca. 1984.

service to the university, a small fraction of which was available when the campus was new.

A record 31,402 students registered for the 2001–2002 school year. In 1925, the vast majority were male; since 1988, most have been female. In addition to the all-male LSU, the all-white LSU is long gone. Today's students are a diverse group, 1,700 of them from other countries. Over 12 percent of the undergraduates are African Americans.

LSU students are also among the state's brightest. Better motivated and goal oriented, these scholars have exhibited a strong desire to learn. The average ACT score for incoming freshmen approaches twenty-four. Taking advantage of the governor's initiative and further enhancing their IT skills, students recently self-imposed a Student Technology Fee to help provide and update technological support on campus. Future graduates will be far better prepared to face the challenges of an IT-based workplace.

LSU serves far beyond the state line. LSU's fire- and police-training schools are utilized by communities throughout the nation, and Mary Manhein's FACES Laboratory helps in the search for missing persons via facial reconstruction from remains. The university's worldwide reach also includes LSU scientists helping to

eradicate hoof-and-mouth disease in the United Kingdom.

With so many current opportunities and more on the horizon, the university community on its Diamond Jubilee had every reason to be confident about the future. Then came Tuesday morning, September 11, 2001. Within a few short minutes, life all over America changed forever, and a determined LSU community joined the country's rise to a new challenge.

Mike the Mascot takes the band through its paces during halftime performance.

New graduates celebrate enthusiastically on the Assembly Center's floor.

2000

LSU baseball team wins the College World Series for the fifth time during the 1990s. Women's track and field team wins its twelfth national championship.

2001

LSU celebrates the seventy-fifth anniversary of the dedication of the present campus.

2001

The Alumni Association opens the Lod and Carole Cook Hotel and Conference Center.

Kayaking on University
Lake.

LSU Union *(left)*

French House

137

Students studying in the
LSU Union.

Springtime in the Quad,
Audubon Hall.

One of the newer buildings
on campus, the Fred C. Frey
Computing Services Center
is built in a style reminiscent
of the campus's original architecture.

East Campus
Apartments

LSU plays Rice, 1995

A view of the Quad from the
Campanile *(right)*.

LSU War Memorial

From Jubilee . . .

Chancellor Mark A. Emmert and LSU System president William L. Jenkins accompany Elizabeth Dole, principal speaker for the festivities to celebrate the Diamond Jubilee of the campus on April 26, 2001.

The springtime finale of yearlong events marking LSU's seventy-five years on this campus included inspiring music and words and dramatic cannon fire.

. . . to Defiant Confidence

"LSU Salutes," held each fall in conjunction with Veterans Day, recognizes LSU's proud military tradition, its fallen servicemen, and its contemporary military students.

Epilogue

On September 11, 2001, two highjacked airliners smashed into the World Trade Center; another crashed in rural Pennsylvania.

The fourth rammed the Pentagon, killing an LSU alumnus on active duty there—Navy Lieutenant Michael "Scotty" Lamana. Back in New York, an estimated twenty-five firefighters and police officers trained by LSU lost their lives in the heroic rescue efforts at the remains of the World Trade Center.

Soon after the attacks of September 11, the federal government granted funds to LSU's Academy of Counter-Terrorist Education (ACE) to train law enforcement personnel to better respond to biological and other forms of terrorism.

And new developments in the war against terrorism continued. Some LSU students saw their education disrupted as the reserve and national guard called up more units to active duty. Yet, in spite of the national tragedy and trauma, there remained an air of confidence on the campus; indeed to some, a defiant confidence.

Yes, LSU's *esprit de corps* lives on in the continuing significance of its tradition as the "Ole War Skule."

Appendix

Louisiana State University Chief Executive Officers

Seminary of Learning of the State of Louisiana (1853–1860)

SUPERINTENDENT

William Tecumseh Sherman, 1859–1860

Louisiana State Seminary of Learning and Military Academy (1860–1870)

SUPERINTENDENTS

William Tecumseh Sherman, 1860–1861
George W. Lay, 1861*
William B. Boggs, 1861*
Anthony Vallas, 1861–1862
W. E. M. Littlefield, 1862–1863
William A. Seay, 1863
Seminary closed (1863–1865)
David French Boyd, 1865–1870

Louisiana State University (1870–1877)

SUPERINTENDENT

David French Boyd, 1870–1877

Louisiana State Agricultural and Mechanical College (1874–1875)

PRESIDENTS

Thomas Nicholson, 1874
Jesse L. Cross, 1874–1875

Louisiana Agricultural and Mechanical College (1875–1877)

PRESIDENT

Jesse L. Cross, 1875–1877

Louisiana State University and Agricultural and Mechanical College (1877–)

PRESIDENTS

David French Boyd, 1877–1880; 1884–1886
William P. Johnston, 1880–1883
James W. Nicholson, 1883–1884; 1887–1896
Thomas D. Boyd, 1886–1887; 1896–1927
Thomas W. Atkinson, 1927–1930
James Monroe Smith, 1930–1939
E. S. Richardson, 1939
Paul M. Hebert, 1939–1941
Campbell B. Hodges, 1941–1944
William B. Hatcher, 1944–1947
Fred C. Frey, 1947
Harold W. Stoke, 1947–1951
Troy H. Middleton, 1951–1962
John A. Hunter, 1962–1965

CHANCELLORS

Cecil G. "Pete" Taylor, 1965–1974
Paul W. Murrill, 1974–1981
Otis B. Wheeler, 1981
James H. Wharton, 1981–1989
E. Grady Bogue, 1989
William E. "Bud" Davis, 1989–1996
William L. Jenkins, 1996–1999
Mark A. Emmert, 1999–

Louisiana State University System (1965–)

PRESIDENTS

John A. Hunter, 1965–1972
Martin D. Woodin, 1972–1985
Allen A. Copping, 1985–1999
William L. Jenkins, 1999–

*Appointed and accepted but never served due to Confederate army obligations

Index

Credits

The photographs in the book, unless noted otherwise, are from the Louisiana State University Photograph Collection, RG#A5000, Louisiana State University Archives, LSU Libraries, Baton Rouge, Louisiana. Photographs from other specific collections are as follows:

Jasper Ewing & Sons Photograph Files, Mss. 3141, Louisiana and Lower Mississippi Valley Collections, LSU Libraries, Baton Rouge, La. The photographs from this collection appear on pages 46, 76, and 77.

David King Gleason Papers and Photograph Collection, Louisiana and Lower Mississippi Valley Collections, LSU Libraries, Baton Rouge, La. The photograph from this collection appears on page 117 and is used with the permission of Josie Gleason.

Eleanor Lobdell Photograph Collection, Mss. 4572, Louisiana and Lower Mississippi Valley Collections, LSU Libraries, Baton Rouge, La. The photograph from this collection appears on page 41.

Huey Long Collection, Mss. 2005, Louisiana and Lower Mississippi Valley Collections, LSU Libraries, Baton Rouge, La. The photograph from this collection appears on page 69.

LSU Libraries, Louisiana Collection Vertical File Photographs, Mss. 4262, Louisiana and Lower Mississippi Valley Collections, LSU Libraries, Baton Rouge, La. The photograph from this collection appears on page 83.

Andrew D. Lytle Collection, Mss. 893, 1254, Louisiana and Lower Mississippi Valley Collections, LSU Libraries, Baton Rouge, La. Photographs from this collection appear on pages 8, 10, 12, 19, 21, 22, 24, 25, 29, 32, 35, and 43.

Alvin E. Rabenhorst Photograph Collection, Mss. 4110, Louisiana and Lower Mississippi Valley Collections, LSU Libraries, Baton Rouge, La. Photographs from this collection appear on pages 13 and 27.

J. E. Snee, Sr. Photograph Collection, Mss. 4069, Louisiana and Lower Mississippi Valley Collections, LSU Libraries, Baton Rouge, La. The photograph from this collection appears on page 30.

Photographs by Fonville Winans (pages 85, 95, and 97) appear with the permission of Bob Winans.

Photographs from the Louisiana State Library (pages 57, 59, 64, 65, 72, 75, 76, 77, 81, 82, 84, 86, 87, and 93) were selected with the generous assistance of Charles East.

In addition, images by Jim Zietz, LSU University Relations, appear on pages ii-iii, v, vi, xii, 102, 105 (both photographs), 116, 127, 136 (both photographs), 138–144, 145 (both photographs), 146 (top), 148, and 162. Images by Prather Warren, LSU University Relations, appear on pages 146 (bottom) and 147 (both photographs).

The assistance of numerous other sources for photographs credited in the captions is also much appreciated, such as that of LSU Sports Information, the Sea Grant College, the Historic New Orleans Collection, and the National Archives.

Front endsheet: Location of LSU's first home, near Pineville, Louisiana. General Topographic Map, Sheet xx, of the Official Records of the Union and Confederate Armies, 1861–1865.

Back endsheet: From the Map of the Parish of East Baton Rouge, Louisiana, compiled and drawn by A. Kaiser and J. A. Swensson, Civil Engineers, 1895. Detail shows the City of Baton Rouge plan (with site of old campus) and Gartness Plantation (eventual site of new campus).

Acknowledgments

My involvement with *Under Stately Oaks: A Pictorial History of LSU* began in early 1992, when I wrote an eight-part series on the school's history for *LSU Magazine.* For this opportunity, I thank Jackie Bartkiewicz, the magazine's Editor and later Executive Director of University Relations.

This series led to my being asked in late 1994 by L. E. Phillabaum, Director of LSU Press, and Laura F. Lindsay, then chairing the University Commission on the History of LSU, to consider writing the text for an illustrated history of LSU. Not only did I accept, but I have thoroughly enjoyed it. I appreciate their confidence and wish to thank both of them, especially Dr. Lindsay for acting as my mentor during the early stages of the project.

Other members of the commission likewise made themselves available for advice and counsel—notably Faye Phillips, Associate Dean for Special Collections; Paul E. Hoffman, Professor of History; and J. Michael Desmond, Associate Professor of Architecture. I owe a debt of gratitude to my LSU Press editor and current mentor, Maureen G. Hewitt, who was always around when I needed her, and to designer Laura Roubique Gleason, who made the book come to life.

For their outstanding efforts in researching and selecting the photographs, deep appreciation must be expressed to Jo Jackson and Mary Hebert Price, former and current University Archivists, respectively. In her dual role as Director of the T. Harry Williams Center for Oral History, Dr. Price proved valuable in other ways as well.

Assisting them were Sissy Albertine, Image Resources; Angie Pitts Juban, graduate assistant for University Archives; Teresa Bergen, freelance editor and former LSU graduate assistant in history. A special thanks goes to Charles East, who researched photographs at the State Library for our use and gave his time generously in earlier consulting on the project. And credit is due Michael K. Smith for his superb indexing.

Appreciation is likewise extended to the two photographers from University Relations who provided an excellent array of current-day LSU images, Jim Zietz, Assistant Director, and Prather Warren. Jim's counsel in the early stages of the project also was invaluable, as was the work of his graduate assistant Amy Connolly.

An outpouring of cooperation came from others on campus—the presidents, chancellors, vice chancellors, deans, department heads, and other members of the faculty, both past and present, and their staff members as well. Dean Billy M. Seay and his Honors College were among the more accommodating.

The staffs at various libraries—including Howard-Tilton at Tulane; Magale at Centenary; Shreve Memorial in Shreveport; the State Library in Baton Rouge; Noel at LSUS; Hill Memorial, Middleton, and the Law Library at LSU; and the Library of Congress in Washington—were always ready to share information. In this, regard, Judy Bolton, head of Public Services at LSU, excelled.

I would also like to thank staff members at the Clerks of Court's offices in Rapides, St. Bernard, and East Baton Rouge Parishes—as well as the Notarial Archives in New Orleans. the National Archives and Records Administration in Washington, The Historic New Orleans Collection, the State Museum in the old New Orleans mint, and the Olmsted Archives in Brookline, Massachusetts.

I also want to recognize Ory Poret, retired director of the State Land Office, for his assistance with the early land grants; Vera Dear with the office of the Board of Regents, who prepared statistical data for me;

J. Stephen Perry, the governor's Chief of Staff, for recapping for me the state's relationship with LSU; and Hope Johns Norman of Alexandria for assistance with the state seminary era.

A sincere thank you also goes to the unsung heroes—friends, relatives, co-workers, and others—-who just wanted to be a part of the book. They performed many mundane but necessary tasks such as proofreading, advising, and challenging my research. Their efforts assisted me far more than they will ever know.

Above all, a special tribute is reserved for the late Steele Burden, who planted LSU's stately oaks in the 1930s for future generations to enjoy.

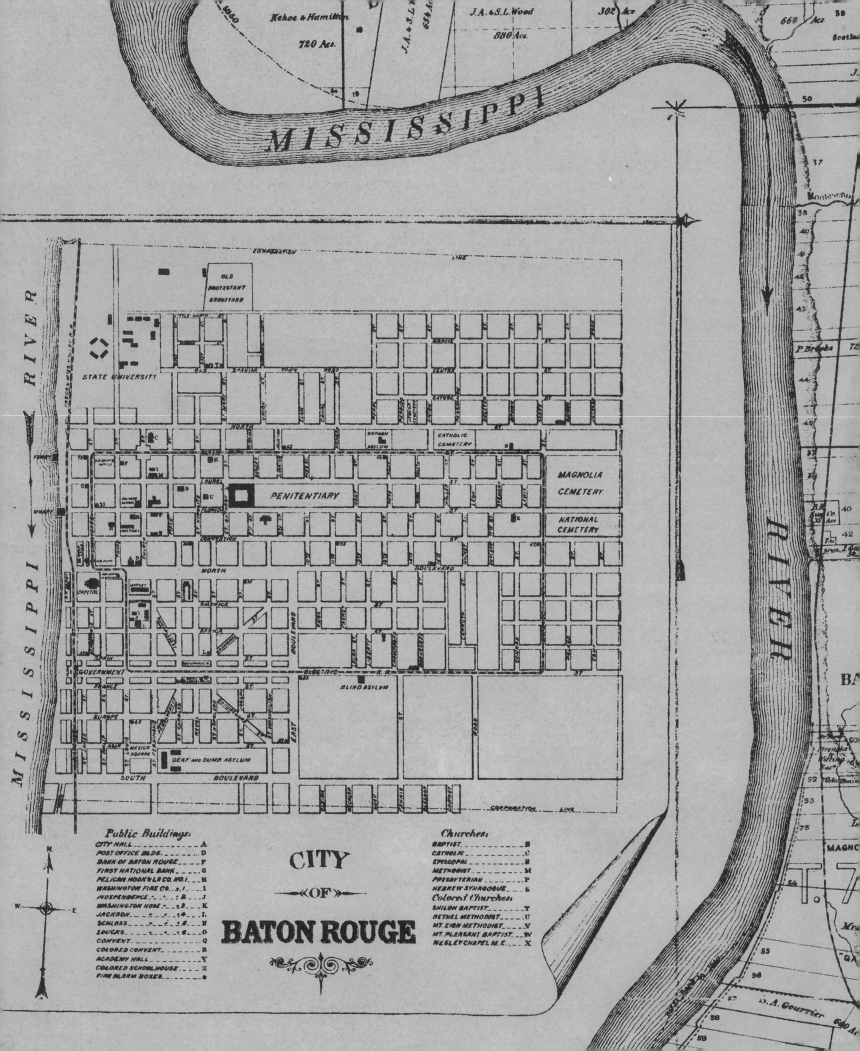

MISSISSIPPI

R I V E R

R I V E R

MISSISSIPPI

Public Buildings:

CITY HALL	A
POST OFFICE BLDG.	D
BANK OF BATON ROUGE	F
FIRST NATIONAL BANK	G
PELICAN HOOK & L.B. CO. NO.1	H
WASHINGTON FIRE CO. 9. 1	I
INDEPENDENCE	J
WASHINGTON HOSE 9	K
JACKSON	L
SCHLOSS	N
LOUCKS	O
CONVENT	Q
COLORED CONVENT	R
ACADEMY HALL	Y
COLORED SCHOOL HOUSE	Z
FIRE ALARM BOXES	●

Churches:

BAPTIST	B
CATHOLIC	C
EPISCOPAL	E
METHODIST	M
PRESBYTERIAN	P
HEBREW SYNAGOGUE	S

Colored Churches:

SHILOH BAPTIST	T
BETHEL METHODIST	U
MT. ZION METHODIST	V
MT. PLEASANT BAPTIST	W
WESLEY CHAPEL M.E.	X

CITY
«OF»
BATON ROUGE